R6473432

39—

1/82

The Biochemistry
of
Psychiatric Disturbances

The Biochemistry
of
Psychiatric Disturbances

Edited by

G. CURZON

Institute of Neurology
University of London

A Wiley–Interscience Publication

JOHN WILEY & SONS
Chichester · New York · Brisbane · Toronto

British Library Cataloguing in Publication Data:

The biochemistry of psychiatric disturbances.
   1. Mental illness–Physiological aspects–Congresses
I. Curzon, G.   II. Biochemical Society.
Neurochemical Group
616.8'9'07   RC455.4.B5   80-40498

ISBN 0 471 27814 9

Typeset by Activity, Teffont, Salisbury, Wilts.
and printed by The Pitman Press, Bath, Avon.

List of Contributors

M. Åsberg   *Psychiatric Clinic, Karolinska Hospital, S-104, 01, Stockholm, Sweden.*

D. M. Bowen   *Department of Neurochemistry, Institute of Neurology, 33 John's Mews, London, WC1N 2NS*

A. Coppen   *Medical Research Council Neuropsychiatric Laboratory, West Park Hospital, Epsom, Surrey, KT19 8PB.*

T. J. Crow   *Division of Psychiatry, Clinical Research Centre, Watford Road, Harrow, Middx., HA1 3UJ.*

G. Curzon   *Department of Neurochemistry, Institute of Neurology, 33 John's Mews, London, WC1N 2NS.*

A. N. Davison   *Department of Neurochemistry, Institute of Neurology, Queen Square, London, WC1N 3BG.*

A. R. Green   *Medical Research Council Clinical Pharmacology Unit, Radcliffe Infirmary, Oxford, OX2 6HE.*

E. G. S. Spokes   *Department of Neurology, Chapel Allerton Hospital, Leeds, LS7 4RB.*

K. Wood   *Medical Research Council Neuropsychiatric Laboratory, West Park Hospital, Epsom, Surrey, KT19 8PB.*

Contents

Abbreviations

CAT	:	Choline acetyltransferase
CSF	:	Cerebrospinal fluid
DA	:	Dopamine
DOPA	:	Dihydroxyphenylalanine
ECS	:	Electroconvulsive shock
ECT	:	Electroconvulsive treatment
GABA	:	γ-Aminobutyric acid
GAD	:	Glutamic acid decarboxylase
5-HIAA	:	5-Hydroxyindoleacetic acid
5-HT	:	5-Hydroxytryptamine
HVA	:	Homovanillic acid
NA	:	Noradrenaline
UFA	:	Unesterified fatty acid

Preface

This volume derives from a meeting organized by the Neurochemical Group of the Biochemical Society held in November 1978 and supported financially by Hoechst UK Ltd and Organon Laboratories Ltd. It summarizes our knowledge of the biochemistry of major psychiatric diseases, mainly describing neurochemical and related therapeutic aspects of depressive illness, of schizophrenia and also of disorders in which consciousness or intellect are impaired—liver failure with central disturbance and Alzheimer's disease. The intention has been to provide a general account by authors who have been closely involved in research in these areas. It is hoped that the volume will be found useful by both specialized research workers and by others in related fields.

Dr Åsberg's chapter deals with the classification of depression and with relationships between antidepressant treatment, transmitter metabolism, and therapeutic outcome. The associations indicated between both suicidal and obsessive–compulsive behaviour and 5-HT metabolism are of particular interest. The chapter by Drs Wood and Coppen centres on brain 5-HT disturbance in endogenous depression and its possible origin. A causal role for 5-HT deficiency receives some support from the therapeutic action of its precursor, tryptophan, when given alone or (less controversially) together with other drugs.

Most effective drug treatments for endogenous depression are to some extent explicable by their influences on 5-HT or other transmitter systems, but until recently there was no convincing evidence that electroconvulsive treatment acted in this way. The work on how electroshock alters behavioural responses to monoamines described by Dr Green permits consideration of its effect on depressive illness in terms of transmitter-based hypotheses. It also illustrates the interrelationships of transmitter systems as it suggests that electroshock alters behavioural responses to catecholamines and 5-HT by decreasing GABA synthesis.

The chapters by Dr Spokes and Dr Crow both concern the DA hypothesis of schizophrenia and focus respectively on neurochemical abnormalities in autopsy material and the effects on symptoms of drugs which release DA or block its receptors. They provide persuasive evidence that hyperactivity of DA-dependent systems is crucial. The location of this disturbance in the brain and its pre- and postsynaptic relationships are questions now generating much research activity. Interest in the roles of other transmitters in schizophrenia is also rising.

The influences on transmitter synthesis of plasma concentrations of precursor amino acids and of their transport to the brain has been appreciated for about a decade but their significance in (for example) depression remains controversial.

Chapter 6, by Curzon, reveals that the increased transport of transmitter precursors to the brain in disorders of liver function can be more readily established and understood, largely because good animal models are available. A number of groups are studying the mechanisms involved and their responsibility for the impairment of consciousness in hepatic encephalopathy. These investigations are leading to new methods of treating the central consequences of liver disease and should encourage neurochemically based research on the effects of other major disturbances of metabolism on consciousness.

Although senile and presenile dementias are such common organic causes of intellectual deterioration, we are only now starting to learn much about the associated neurochemical disturbances. Bowen and Davison describe transmitter and other changes in these disorders. Evidence that the cholinergic system may be particularly impaired is of great interest and suggests possibilities for therapeutic intervention.

The short final chapter discusses some very recent neurochemical findings which may be relevant to psychiatric disease. The importance of emerging evidence on functional relationships between transmitters is emphasized. On the one hand, these complexities make the interpretation of research findings more difficult; on the other, they may point to new approaches to treatment.

Finally, I thank my co-authors for their collaboration and the publishers for their help and patience.

G. Curzon

The Biochemistry of Psychiatric Disturbances
Edited by G. Curzon
© 1980 John Wiley & Sons Ltd.

CHAPTER 1

Biochemical Abnormalities in Depressive Illness: Effects of Drugs

MARIE ÅSBERG

New treatments for illnesses will often lead to increased understanding of their pathophysiology. This has clearly been the case with the tricyclic antidepressants and depressive illness. The present chapter reviews some investigations of the pharmacokinetic and pharmacodynamic properties of these drugs, and resultant investigations into the biochemistry of depression.

THE CONCEPT OF DEPRESSION

An 'antidepressant' drug should presumably have the effect of alleviating depression. Depression is, however, a nebulous concept and the term is used for conditions ranging from normal, transient mood states to long-standing, clearly pathological syndromes with an increased mortality (Avery and Winokur, 1976) and a clear genetic background (Gershon et al., 1976). Tricyclic antidepressants do not alleviate normal sadness. The mood-elevating effects appear to be limited to pathological states, i.e. depressive syndromes. Such syndromes with their characteristic combination of sadness and inner tension, pessimistic thoughts, reduced interest in the surroundings, reduced activity, and appetite and sleep disturbances, are ubiquitous in psychiatry. They are common in the later phases of schizophrenic illness, in alcoholism, and in anxiety states. Although clinicians often prescribe tricyclic antidepressants in these circumstances, their therapeutic effects here are not very well documented. The main indication for tricyclic treatment remains the primary depressive disorders (as defined by Feighner et al., 1972) that occur without any other preceding psychiatric illness.

CLASSIFICATION OF PRIMARY DEPRESSIVE DISORDERS

Clinicians have long been struck by the variability in symptom pattern and course between depressed patients, and a large number of subclassifications of depressive illness have been proposed, e.g. endogenous–reactive, psychotic–neurotic, agitated–

1

retarded, vital–personal, bipolar–unipolar etc. These dichotomies are by no means synonymous with each other and this has led to considerable difficulties in the interpretation of drug studies where different principles of classification have been used. The Research Diagnostic Criteria (RDC) recently proposed by Spitzer *et al.*, (1977) provide carefully defined criteria for some of these classifications and will presumably be very helpful to future researchers.

Statistical multivariate analyses have been used by several investigators (see review by Garside and Roth, 1978) in the hope of finding more valid classification schemes. Most of these investigations suggest that the distinction of 'endogenous' depression is a valid one, insofar as certain symptoms associated with this term do tend to occur together and are also associated with a more favourable response to drugs and to electroconvulsive treatment.

Overall and coworkers (1966) in the United States and Paykel (Paykel, 1971; Paykel and Henderson, 1977) in the United Kingdom performed cluster analyses of depressive illness and found rather similar subgroupings of patients in the two countries. These authors identify three or four subgroups in the American studies called retarded depression, anxious depression, and hostile depression. These three groups seem to react differently to imipramine. Raskin (1974) in a review of a large multihospital study including more than 500 patients reports a significant superiority of imipramine to placebo in retarded depression, equal effects in anxious depression, and a significantly poorer effect of imipramine than placebo in hostile depression.

Roth and colleagues have used multiple regression analyses in a large sample of clinically classified patients with affective disorders and have developed interview-based inventories, where symptoms and signs are given different weights in accordance with their power to discriminate between anxiety states and depressive illness, and between endogenous and reactive depression (Gurney *et al.*, 1972). The inventory scores have the advantage of allowing a high degree of reliability of the diagnostic classification and we have consistently used them in our studies of antidepressant treatment.

RATING SEVERITY OF DEPRESSION

Amelioration of depression with drug treatment is slow, gradual and often incomplete. This means that for a detailed study of drug effects some quantification of severity is needed. In psychiatry, the quantification of pathology is usually accomplished by means of rating scales. A rating scale is a peculiar measuring instrument, which essentially consists of a series of descriptions of phenomena and rules for grading them. The quality of the instrument depends on the clarity of these instructions and also on the selection and description of relevant signs and symptoms.

In comparison with the amount of work done on classification, relatively little attention has been given to increasing the precision of rating. Insufficient sensitivity and accuracy of rating procedures may be one reason why significant differences between beneficial effects of different treatments are so seldom found in clinical trials even when clinicians are convinced that differences exist and the pharmacological profiles of the drugs differ.

Recently, interest in developing more sensitive rating methods has increased. One example of this trend is the Comprehensive Psychopathological Rating Scale (CPRS) (Åsberg et al., 1978a). In contrast to most previous scales, this was explicitly intended for treatment evaluation, and this purpose is reflected in its construction (see Åsberg and Schalling, 1979).

In our studies we have used a depression scale constructed by Cronholm and Ottosson (1960) and more recently the CPRS from which an empirically based subscale for depression has been designed (Montgomery and Åsberg, 1979).

PLASMA LEVELS OF ANTIDEPRESSANT DRUGS

In 1966, it became possible to measure accurately the minute concentrations of tricyclic antidepressant drugs present in plasma during ordinary treatment. An impressive variability of plasma levels was found between individuals who received similar doses of desipramine or nortriptyline (Hammer et al., 1967). In a series of investigations where nortriptyline was used as a model drug, the reasons for, and the consequences of this variability have been explored.

In some of these experiments, Alexanderson and coworkers described the kinetic parameters which determine plasma levels during steady state. Twin studies (Alexanderson et al., 1969) showed a substantial genetic contribution to the steady state level and family studies confirmed this and also suggested a polygenic inheritance (Åsberg et al., 1971a). Also independent genetic control of the two important pharmacokinetic parameters, volume of distribution and elimination half life, has been demonstrated (Alexanderson, 1972). Both these parameters can be measured in repeated blood samples after a single oral dose. The clearance value calculated from them is an extremely accurate predictor of steady state concentration during long-term treatment. These findings suggest that the kinetic parameters are personal characteristics that change little with time unless other drugs are given as well (Sjöqvist el al., 1968; Alexanderson et al., 1969).

The genetic and kinetic studies were performed in healthy volunteers, but the prediction technique opens up possibilities for rapid dosage adjustment in patients. These possibilities have been studied recently by Cooper and Simpson (1978); Braithwaite et al. (1978) and Potter et al. (1978).

PLASMA LEVELS AND CLINICAL EFFECTS

Variability of plasma tricyclic concentration between different subjects might account for some of the variability in antidepressant effect and probably also for some cases of unexpected side-effects. The first drug to be studied intensively for this purpose was nortriptyline.

In our first pilot study on nortriptyline (Åsberg et al., 1971b) there appeared to be a relationship between drug level in plasma and antidepressant effect. This was not of the expected sigmoid type, but had an inverted U-shape. Low plasma levels as well as very high levels appeared to be associated with a decreased effect. This type of 'therapeutic window' relationship for nortriptyline has since been found in several studies (Kragh-Sørensen et al., 1973, 1976; Ziegler et al., 1976; Montgomery et al., 1978). Apart from its obvious clinical importance, it is interesting because it suggests that nortriptyline may have different biochemical actions with different dose–response curves and different consequences for the mood state. It is not known what additional effect occurs at high nortriptyline levels and reduces therapeutic benefit, but a receptor blocking action has been suggested. The observation of Coppen and Ghose (1978) of a strong association between poor therapeutic effects of nortriptyline and reduced sensitivity to the pressor effects of phenylephrine (a direct α-adrenoceptor agonist) in subjects with high nortriptyline levels would support this interpretation. A central anticholinergic effect, or a histamine receptor blocking effect are other possibilities.

With imipramine the relationship between plasma level and therapeutic effect appears to be linear (Reisby et al., 1977; Glassman et al., 1977). For amitriptyline (which is demethylated to nortriptyline in the body) the situation is less clear. In the study where very high plasma levels were reached, there seemed to be a diminished therapeutic effect with very high concentrations of this drug (Montgomery et al., 1978).

There has been much conflict over the importance of plasma levels of tricylic antidepressants as predictors of their therapeutic effects. Different results may to some extent depend on differences in patient selection and methodology (for discussion, see Åsberg and Sjöqvist 1978). The correlations found are usually rather low and thus easily missed when less sensitive methods are used. There may also be pharmacological reasons for the relative weakness of the correlations observed. The two-to-fourfold variability in protein binding of tricyclics between individuals (Alexanderson and Borgå, 1972; Glassman et al., 1973, Bertilsson et al., 1979; Potter et al., 1979b) may have weakened the apparent correlations between drug levels and therapeutic effect, since only the total, and not the unbound drug (which is the pharmacologically active fraction) was measured. Another reason for low correlation is that hydroxylated metabolites, previously thought to be inactive, may contribute to the effect of these drugs on central NAergic neurons (Siwers et al., 1977; Potter et al., 1979a; Bertilsson et al., 1979b).

BIOCHEMICAL EFFECTS OF THE TRICYCLIC ANTIDEPRESSANTS

All tricyclic antidepressants inhibit transmitter uptake in NA neurons, either directly or by means of active metabolites. A few of them, in particular clomipramine, are also 5-HT uptake inhibitors. 5-HT uptake inhibition with this drug is a function of the concentration of the parent compound (Träskman et al., 1979a).

Its main metabolite, demethylclomipramine, is a potent inhibitor of NA uptake. Treatment with clomipramine can therefore be expected to have effects on both systems. When the drug is given by mouth, the concentration of the metabolite during steady state is usually much higher than that of the parent compound but there is a substantial variability between patients in the ratio between the two.

Inhibition of transmitter reuptake is believed to potentiate transmitter function and this in turn leads to a feedback reduction of transmitter synthesis. This is probably the reason why transmitter metabolite concentrations in the CSF decrease during treatment with tricyclic antidepressants. In depressed patients treated with clomipramine, the decrease in the NA metabolite, 4-hydroxy-3-methoxyphenyl glycol (HMPG) correlated with the plasma level of the demethyl metabolite. The reduction in the 5-HT metabolite, 5-HIAA in the CSF is strongly correlated to the 5-HT uptake measured *in vitro* in plasma from treated patients (Åsberg *et al.*, 1977). It is also correlated with the concentration of clomipramine in plasma, but only up to a certain level (Träskman *et al.*, 1979) above which there is little effect on CSF 5-HIAA. This may indicate 5-HT receptor blockade with higher concentrations of this drug tending to affect 5-HT metabolism in the opposite direction (Thorén *et al.*, 1980).

PRETREATMENT CSF LEVELS OF MONOAMINE METABOLITES

The fact that antidepressant drugs interfere with monoamine transmission has led to the hypothesis of deranged monoamine function in depressive illness (Schildkraut, 1965; Lapin and Oxenkrug, 1969). To obtain direct information on monoamine neurons in the brain of a living patient is obviously very difficult and several indirect approaches have therefore been used (see review by Murphy and coworkers, 1978). One way is to measure concentrations of amine metabolites in CSF. Although there are many potential sources of error with this technique, there have been several reports of lower metabolite levels in depressives than in controls, in particular of the 5-HT metabolite, 5-HIAA (e.g. Dencker *et al.*, 1966; Ashcroft *et al.*, 1966; Coppen *et al.*, 1972; van Praag *et al.*, 1973). These earlier investigators used spectrophotoflurometric assessment methods, which may be of too low sensitivity and accuracy, unless the concentration of the metabolite is raised by blocking its egress from CSF by probenecid administration (Sjöqvist and Johansson, 1978).

Using mass fragmentographic determinations of CSF 5-HIAA it has been possible to confirm the earlier findings of reduced levels in depressed patients (Åsberg *et al.*, 1978b, Åsberg and Bertilsson, 1979). The difference between depressives and controls is, however, not very marked. What may be more important is that the CSF 5-HIAA concentrations in depressive illness appear to be bimodally distributed (Åsberg *et al.*, 1973, 1976a) so that about 30% of the patients occupy the lower mode (with 5-HIAA levels below 15 ng ml^{-1} CSF). This finding suggests the existence of biochemical subgroups within the endogenous depressive syndrome.

PRETREATMENT CSF 5-HIAA AND TREATMENT OUTCOME

Since nortriptyline is a preferential NA uptake blocker with little effect on 5-HT neurons (Bertilsson *et al.*, 1974), it was not surprising that it appeared to be less effective in patients with low pretreatment levels of CSF 5-HIAA (Åsberg *et al.*, 1973). If a low CSF 5-HIAA concentration reflects a disturbance of central 5-HT turnover, a 5-HT uptake blocker might have better therapeutic effect.

Studies with clomipramine (Träskman *et al.*, 1979) have, however, not given a clearcut answer to this question, probably in part because of the mixed neuronal effects of the compound. In patients with a normal pretreatment 5-HIAA, the antidepressant effect was strongly correlated ($r = 0.65$, $p < 0.01$) to the plasma concentrations, not of the compound itself but to those of its demethylated metabolite which (as we have seen) interferes with NA reuptake. The antidepressant effect also correlated with CSF concentrations of the NA metabolite HMPG ($r = 0.54$, $p < 0.05$). These results suggest that in these depressives, the effect on NA neurons mediates the antidepressant action.

In patients with low pretreatment 5-HIAA, therapeutic benefit did not correlate with CSF 5-HIAA reduction, CSF HMPG reduction, plasma concentrations of clomipramine, or with those of its metabolite. That potentiation of 5-HT function may nonetheless be important is suggested by the findings of Wålinder *et al.* (1976) who potentiated the effects of clomipramine by adding the 5-HT precursor amino acid tryptophan.

There is also evidence that 5-HT uptake inhibition may be beneficial in another psychiatric illness, obsessive–compulsive disorder. Clomipramine has a significantly better effect than placebo in this very intractable illness (Thorén *et al.*, 1979a; I. M. Marks *et al.*, 1980). The anti-obsessive effect is strongly correlated to the reduction of 5-HIAA in spinal fluid (Thorén *et al.*, 1980). Somewhat surprisingly there is a strong negative correlation between clomipramine in plasma and anti-obsessive effect. The explanation for this is that patients with obsessive-compulsive disorder had higher plasma levels than depressives. They thus tended to lie on the right hand limb of the 'U' which describes the correlation between plasma level of clomipramine and 5-HIAA in spinal fluid during treatment.

Also in obsessive–compulsive disorder a low pretreatment 5-HIAA was associated with a significantly poorer effect of clomipramine. Perhaps normally functioning 5-HT neurons are a prerequisite for a therapeutic effect of 5-HT uptake inhibition.

CSF 5-HIAA AND SUICIDE

The finding of a bimodal distribution of pretreatment 5-HIAA in CSF from depressed patients encouraged us to search for clinical correlates of the metabolite levels. Although there were no clearcut differences in severity or symptom profile between the patients in the two 5-HIAA modes (below and above 15 ng ml^{-1}, respectively), there was an apparent association between a low 5-HIAA level and suicide attempts.

Some 40% of the patients with a low level of CSF 5-HIAA had attempted suicide, in contrast to 15% of those with high 5-HIAA levels (Åsberg et al., 1976b).

The association between a low CSF 5-HIAA and suicidal behaviour has recently been confirmed in a new group of 30 patients who were hospitalized after a suicide attempt (Träskman et al., 1980b). Most of these patients were not clinically depressed. There was no evidence of bimodality of the 5-HIAA distribution in these patients, and its distribution in 45 healthy volunteer controls also appeared normal. The suicide attempters had, however, significantly lower 5-HIAA levels than the controls, and the difference (which could not be accounted for by age or sex differences) was more pronounced for those who had made violent suicide attempts.

In a one year follow-up study of suicide attempters, the mortality was found to be alarmingly high. Six out of 46 suicide attempters had died from suicide, and all of these had previously shown 5-HIAA levels in CSF below the median of all patients.

CSF 5-HIAA AND CSF CORTISOL

Although most research on suicide has focused on demographic, social, or psychological factors, a few investigators have also examined biological variables. Among these are two studies by Bunney and coworkers in 1965, who found an association between suicidal behaviour and a high excretion of 17-hydroxycorticosteroids in urine. Since 5-HT neurons are thought to be involved in the control of ACTH secretion, we examined the possible relationship between CSF 5-HIAA and CSF cortisol. Although we confirmed the findings of Carroll and associates (1976) of raised CSF cortisol in endogenous depression, we found normal concentrations in suicide attempters, and no correlation with CSF 5-HIAA (Träskman et al., 1980a).

CSF 5-HIAA AND PLATELET MAO

Another biological variable which seems consistently related to suicide is a low monoamine oxidase activity in blood platelets (Buchsbaum et al., 1976, 1977; Sullivan et al., 1979; Gottfries et al., 1980) and in brain (Gottfries et al., 1975). Low MAO activity has also been associated with alcoholism (Buchsbaum et al., 1976; Wiberg et al., 1977; Sullivan et al., 1979). Ballenger et al. (1979) have recently shown lower levels of CSF 5-HIAA in abstinent alcoholics than in non-alchoholic psychiatric controls. This suggests that the two variables may reflect a common underlying factor (5-HT transmission?) which may be associated with vulnerability to a range of psychiatric disturbances. There appears to be no correlation between platelet MAO activity and CSF 5-HIAA in any of the patient groups studied by us (suicide attempters, currently depressed patients, recovered depressives), but in healthy controls, a positive correlation was demonstrated (L. Oreland, Å. Wiberg, M. Åsberg, L. Träskman, L. Sjöstrand, P. Thorén, L. Bertilsson, and G. Tybring, submitted). A possible explanation may be that platelet MAO, which is known to be under relatively strong genetic control, tends to reflect more enduring characteristics of the 5-HT system, while 5-HIAA in CSF tends to reflect its temporary state. Although 5-HIAA concentrations in healthy controls seem to remain fairly stable over limited periods, some depressed patients with low levels show a significant increase when recovered and off drugs (Åsberg and Bertilsson, 1979; M. Åsberg and L. Bertilsson, unpublished data). The changes in CSF 5-HIAA with drug administration are also consistent with this explanation.

CONCLUDING REMARKS

Although the mechanism of action of the tricyclic antidepressant is still controversial, it seems plausible that some aspect of their interference with monoaminergic functions in the central nervous system is of importance. Whether it is the uptake inhibition or possible consequences such as altered receptor sensitivity or other neuronal adjustments is not yet known. Whatever the mechanism of action may be, there is now satisfactory evidence that it depends on an adequate concentration of the drug at its receptor, and that the concentration in plasma is a better indicator of this than the ingested dose. Comparatively simple monitoring techniques can thus be used to increase the efficacy of treatment.

The discovery of the uptake inhibiting properties of the antidepressants provided part of the background for the formulation of the 'catecholamine hypothesis' and the 'indoleamine hypothesis' of the affective disorders. Although most investigators recognize the limitations of these hypotheses, they continue to inspire research in depression. At present it seems that disturbances of monoaminergic functions are of importance for psychiatric disorders, but perhaps more as predisposing factors associated with an increased vulnerability to a wide range of psychiatric disturbances. This may open new possibilities for treatment and prophylaxis. Drugs with specific effects on 5-HT or NA neurons are already available. It is also conceivable that if psychological correlates of e.g. disturbed 5-HT turnover could be identified, such knowledge might provide the foundation for more specific psychotherapeutic intervention than has hitherto been possible.

ACKNOWLEDGEMENTS

The work reviewed in this chapter has received support from the Swedish Medical Research Council (29X-5015, 4X-3902, 21P-4676, and 21X-5454), the Gurli Wehtje Fund for Research in Depression and by funds from the Karolinska Institute.

REFERENCES

Alexanderson, B. (1972) Pharmacokinetics of nortriptyline in man after single and multiple oral doses: the predictability of steady state plasma concentrations from single dose plasma level data. *European Journal of Clinical Pharmacology,* **4**, 82-91.

Alexanderson, B., and Borgå, O. (1972) Interindividual differences in plasma protein binding of nortriptyline in man—a twin study. *European Journal of Clinical Pharmacology,* **4**, 196-200.

Alexanderson, B., Evans, D. A. P., and Sjöqvist, F. (1969) Steady state plasma levels of nortriptyline in twins. Influence of genetic factors and drug therapy. *British Medical Journal,* **iv**, 764-768.

Åsberg, M., and Bertilsson, L. (1979) Serotonin in depressive illness—studies of CSF 5-HIAA, in Saletu, B. (ed.) *Proceedings of the 11th CINP Congress Vienna 1978,* Pergamon Press, New York, (in press).

Åsberg, M., and Schalling, D. (1979) Construction of a new psychiatric rating instrument, the Comprehensive Psychopathological Rating Scale (CPRS). *Progress in Neuropsychopharmacology,* **3**, (in press).

Åsberg, M., and Sjöqvist, F., (1978) On the role of plasma level monitoring of tricyclic antidepressants in clinical practice, *Communications in Psychopharmacology,* **2**, 381-391.

Åsberg, M., Evans, D. A. P., and Sjöqvist, F. (1971a) Genetic control of nortriptyline kinetics in man: a study of relatives of propositi with high plasma concentrations, *Journal of Medical Genetics,* **8**, 129-135.

Åsberg, M. Cronholm, B., Sjöqvist, F., and Tuck, D. (1971b) Relationship between plasma level and therapeutic effect of nortriptyline, *British Medical Journal,* **iii**, 331-334.

Åsberg, M., Bertilsson, L., Tuck, D., Cronholm, B., and Sjöqvist, F. (1973) Indoleamine metabolites in the cerebrospinal fluid of depressed patients before and during treatment with nortriptyline. *Clinical Pharmacology and Therapeutics,* **14**, 277-286.

Åsberg, M., Thorén, P., Träskman, L., Bertilsson, B., and Ringberger, V. (1976a) Serotonin depression—a biochemical supgroup within the affective disorders. *Science,* **191**, 478-480.

Åsberg, M., Träskman, L., and Thorén, P. (1976b) 5-HIAA in the cerebrospinal fluid—a biochemical suicide predictor? *Archives of General Psychiatry,* **33**, 1193-1197.

Åsberg, M., Ringberger, V.-A., Sjöqvist, F. Thorén, P., Träskman, L., and Tuck, J. R. (1977) Monoamine metabolites in cerebrospinal fluid and serotonin uptake inhibition during treatment with chlorimipramine. *Clinical Pharmacology and Therapeutics,* **21**, 201-207.

Åsberg, M., Bertilsson, L., Thorén, P., and Träskman, L. (1978b) CSF monoamine metabolites in depressive illness, in Garattini, S. (ed.) *Depressive disorders: Symposium in Rome May 9-11 1977* Schattauer, Stuttgart, New York, pp. 293-305.

Åsberg, M., Montgomery, S., Perris, C., Schalling, D., and Sedvall, G. (1978a) The Comprehensive Psychopathological Rating Scale (CPRS). *Acta psychiatrica Scandinavica,* **Suppl. 271**, 5-27.

Ashcroft, G. W., Crawford, T. B. B., Eccleston, D., Sharman, D. F., McDougall, E. J., Stanton, J. B., and Binns, J. K. (1966) 5-Hydroxyindole compounds in the cerebrospinal fluid of patients with psychiatric or neurological diseases. *Lancet,* **ii**, 1049-1052.

Avery, D., and Winokur, G. (1976) Mortality in depressed patients treated with electroconvulsive therapy and antidepressants. *Archives of General Psychiatry,* **33**, 1029-1037.

Ballenger, J. C., Goodwin, F. K., Major, L. F., and Brown, G. L. (1979) Alcohol and central serotonin metabolism in man. *Archives of General Psychiatry*, **36**, 224–227.

Bertilsson, L., Åsberg, M., and Thorén, P. (1974) Differential effect of chlorimipramine and nortriptyline on cerebrospinal fluid metabolites of serotonin and noradrenaline in depression. *European Journal of clinical Pharmacology*, **7**, 365–368.

Bertilsson, L., Braithwaite, R., Tybring, G., Carle, M., and Borgå, D. (1979a) Plasma protein binding of demethyl-chlorimipramine studied with various techniques. *Clinical Pharmacology and Therapeutics*, **26**, 265–271.

Bertillson, L., Mellström, B., and Sjöqvist, F. (1979b) Pronounced inhibition of noradrenaline uptake by 10-hydroxy-metabolites of nortriptyline, *Life Sciences*, **25**, 1285–1292.

Braithwaite, R., Montgomery, S., and Dawling, S. (1978) Nortriptyline in depressed patients with high plasma levels. *Clinical Pharmacology and Therapeutics*, **23**, 303–308.

Buchsbaum, M. S., Coursey, R. D., and Murphy, D. L. (1976) The biochemical high-risk paradigm: behavioral and genetical correlates of low platelet monoamine oxidase activity. *Science*, **194**, 339–341.

Buchsbaum, M. S., Haier, R. J., and Murphy, D. L. (1977) Suicide attempts, platelet monoamine oxidase and the average evoked response. *Acta psychiatrica scandinavica*, **56**, 69–79.

Bunney, W. E., Jr., and Fawcett, J. A. (1965) Possibility of a biochemical test for suicidal potential. *Archives of General Psychiatry*, **13**, 232–239.

Bunney, W. E., Jr., Fawcett, J. A., Davis, J. M., and Gifford, S. (1965) Further evaluation of urinary 17-hydroxycorticosteroids in suicidal patients. *Archives of General Psychiatry*, **21**, 138–150.

Carroll, B. J., Curtis, G. C., and Mendels, J. (1976) Cerebrospinal fluid and plasma free cortisol concentrations in depression. *Psychological Medicine*, **6**, 235–244.

Cooper, T. B., and Simpson, G. M. (1978) Prediction of individual dosage of nortriptyline. *American Journal of Psychiatry*, **135**, 333–335.

Coppen, A., and Ghose, K. (1978) Peripheral α-adrenoceptor and central dopamine receptor activity in depressive patients. *Psychopharmacology*, **59**, 171–177.

Coppen, A., Prange, A. J., Whybrow, P. C., and Noguera, R. (1972) Abnormalities of indolamines in affective disorders. *Archives of General Psychiatry*, **26**, 474–478.

Cronholm, B., and Ottosson, J.-O. (1960) Experimental studies of the therapeutic action of electroconvulsive therapy in endogenous depression. *Acta psychiatrica scandinavica*, **35**, suppl 145, 69–101.

Dencker, S. J., Malm, U., Roos, B.-E., and Werdinius, B. (1966) Acid monoamine metabolites of cerebrospinal fluid in mental depression and mania. *Journal of Neurochemistry*, **13**, 1545–1548.

Feighner, J. P., Robins, E., Guze, S. B., Woodruff, R. A., Jr., Winokur, G., and Munoz, R. (1972) Diagnostic criteria for use in psychiatric research. *Archives of General Psychiatry*, **26**, 57–63.

Garside, R. F., and Roth, M. (1978) Multivariate statistical methods and problems of classification in psychiatry. *British Journal of Psychiatry*, **133**, 53–67.

Gershon, E. S., Bunney, W. E., Jr., Leckman, J. F., Van Eerdewegh, M., and DeBauche, B. A. (1976) The inheritance of affective disorders: a review of data and hypotheses. *Behavior Genetics*, **6**, 227–261.

Glassman, A. H., Hurwic, M. J., and Perel, J. M. (1973) Plasma binding of imipramine and clinical outcome. *American Journal of Psychiatry*, **130**, 1367–1369.

Glassman, A. H., Perel, J. M., Shostak, M., Kantor, S. J., and Fleiss, J. L. (1977) Clinical implications of imipramine plasma levels for depressive illness. *Archives of General Psychiatry*, **34**, 197–204.

Gottfries, C.-G., Von Knorring, L., and Oreland, L. (1980) Platelet monoamine oxidase activity in mental disorders. 2. Affective psychoses and suicidal behaviour. *Progress in Neuro-psycho pharmacology* (in press).

Gottfries, C.-G., Oreland, L., Wiberg, Å., and Winblad, B. (1975) Lowered monoamine oxidase activity in brains from alcoholic suicides. *Journal of Neurochemistry*, **25**, 667–673.

Gurney, C., Roth, M., Garside, R. F., Kerr, T. A., and Schapira, K. (1972) Studies in the classification of affective disorders. The relationship between anxiety states and depressive illnesses—II. *British Journal of Psychiatry*, **121**, 162–166.

Hammer, W., Ideström, C.-M., and Sjöqvist, F. (1967) Chemical control of antidepressant drug therapy, in Garattini, S., and Dukes, M. N. G. (eds.) in *Proceedings of the First International Symposium on Antidepressant drugs* Excerpta Medica International Congress Series, No. 122, Excerpta Medica, Amsterdam, pp. 301–310.

Kragh-Sørensen, P., Hansen, C. E., and Åsberg, M. (1973) Plasma levels of nortriptyline in the treatment of endogenous depression. *Acta psychiatrica scandinavica*, **49**, 444–456.

Kragh-Sørensen, P., Eggert-Hansen, C., Baastrup, P. C., and Hvidberg, E. F. (1976) Self-inhibiting action of nortriptyline's antidepressive effect at high plasma levels. *Psychopharmacologia*, **45**, 305–316.

Lapin, I. P., and Oxenkrug, C. F. (1969) Intensification of the central serotoninergic processes as a possible determinant of the thymoleptic effect. *Lancet*, i, 132–136.

Marks, I. M., Stern, R. S., Mawson, D., Cobb, J. and McDonald, R. (1980) Clomipramine and exposure for obsessive-compulsive ritual. *British Journal of Psychiatry*, **136**, 1–25.

Montgomery, S., and Åsberg, M. (1979) A new depression scale designed to be sensitive to change. *British Journal of Psychiatry*, **134**, 382–389.

Montgomery, S., Braithwaite, B., Dawling, S., and McAuley, R. (1978) High plasma nortriptyline levels in the treatment of depression. *Clinical Pharmacology and Therapeutics*, **23**, 309–314.

Murphy, D. L., Campbell, I. C., and Costa, J. L. (1978) The brain serotonergic system in the affective disorders. *Progress in Neuropsychopharmocology*, **2**, 1–31.

Overall, J. E., Hollister, L. E., Johnson, M., and Pennington, V. (1966) Nosology of depression and differential response to drugs, *Journal of the American Medical Association*, **195**, 946–948.

Paykel, E. S. (1971) Classification of depressed patients: a cluster analysis derived grouping. *British Journal of Psychiatry*, **118**, 275–288.

Paykel, E. S., and Henderson, A. J. (1977) Application of cluster analysis in the classification of depression. *Neuropsychobiology*, **3**, 111–119.

Potter, W. Z., Zavadil, A. P., and Goodwin, F. K. (1978a) Prediction of steady state plasma concentration of impramine. *Psychopharmacology Bulletin*, **14**, 29–33.

Potter, W. Z., Muscettola, G., and Goodwin, G. K. (1979b) Binding of imipramine to plasma protein and brain tissue: relationship to CSF tricyclic levels in man. *Psychopharmacology*, **63**, 187–192.

Potter, W. Z., Calil, H. M., Manian, A. A., Zavadil, A. P., and Goodwin, F. K. (1979a) Hydroxylated metabolites of tricyclic antidepressants: preclinical assessment of activity. *Biological Psychiatry*, **14**, 601–613.

van Praag, H. M., Korf, J., and Schut, D. (1973) Cerebral monoamines and depression. *Archives of General Psychiatry*, **28**, 827–831.

Raskin, A. (1974) A guide for drug use in depressive disorders. *American Journal of Psychiatry*, **131**, 181–185.

Reisby, N., Gram, L. F., Beck, P., Nagy, A., Petersen, G. O., Ortmann, J., Ibsen, I., Dencker, S. J., Jacobsen, O., Krantweld, O., Sondergaard, I., and Christiansen, J. (1977) Imipramine: clinical effects and pharmacokinetic variability. *Psychopharmacology*, **54**, 263–272.

Schildkraut, J. J. (1965) The catecholamine hypothesis of affective disorders. A review of supporting evidence. *American Journal of Psychiatry*, **122**, 509–522.

Siwers, B., Borg, S., d'Elia, G., Lundin, G., Plym Forshell, G., Raotma, H., and Roman, G. (1977) Comparative clinical evaluation of lofepramine and imipramine. Pharmacological aspects. *Acta psychiatrica Scandinavica*, **55**, 21–31.

Sjöqvist, B., and Johansson, B. (1978) A comparison between fluorometric and mass fragmentographic determinations of homovanillic acid and 5-hydroxyindoleacetic acid in human cerebrospinal fluid. *Journal of Neurochemistry*, **31**, 621–625.

Sjöqvist, F., Hammer, W., Ideström, C.-M., Lind, M., Tuck, D., and Åsberg, M. (1968) Plasma level of monomethylated tricyclic antidepressants and side-effects in man, in *Toxicity and side-effects of psychotropic drugs*, Excerpta Medica International Congress Series, No. 145, Excerpta Medica, Amsterdam, pp. 246–257.

Spitzer, R. L., Endicott, J., and Robins, E. (1977) *Research Diagnostic Criteria (RDC) for a selected group of functional disorders*. (3rd Edn.) National Institute of Mental Health, Bethesda, Md.

Sullivan, J. L., Cavenar, J. O., Maltbie, A. A., Lister, P., and Zung, W. W. K. (1979) Familial biochemical and clinical correlates of alcoholics with low platelet monoamine oxidase activity. *Biological Psychiatry*, **14**, 385–394.

Thorén, P., Åsberg, M., Cronholm, B., Jörnestedt, L., and Träskman, L. (1980a) Chlorimipramine treatment of obsessivecompulsive disorder. I. A controlled clinical trial. *Archives of General Psychiatry* (in press).

Thorén, P., Åsberg, M., Bertilsson, L., Mellström, B., Sjöqvist, F., and Träskman, L. (1980b) Chlorimipramine treatment of obsessive compulsive disorder. II. Biochemical aspects. *Archives of General Psychiatry* (in press).

Träskman, L. Åsberg, M., Bertilsson, L., Cronholm, B., Mellström, B., Neckers, L. M., Sjöqvist, F., Thorén, P., and Tybring, G. (1979a). Plasma levels of chlorimipramine and its demethylmetabolite during treatment of depression. Differential biochemical and clinical effects of the two compounds. *Clinical Pharmacology and Therapeutics*, (in press).

Träskman, L., Tybring, G., Åsberg, M., Bertilsson, L., Lantto, O., and Schalling, D. (1980a), CSF cortisol in depressed and suicide patients. *Archives of General Psychiatry* (in press).

Träskman, L., Åsberg, M., Bertilsson, L., and Sjöstrand, L. (1980b) Monoamine metabolites in cerebrospinal fluid and suicidal behaviour. *Archives of General Psychiatry* (in press).

Wålinder, J., Skott, A., Carlsson, A., Nagy, A., and Roos, B.-E. (1976) Potentiation of the antidepressant action of clomipramine by tryptophan. *Archives of General Psychiatry*, **33**, 1384–1389.

Wiberg, Å., Gottfries, C.-G., and Oreland, L. (1977) Low platelet monoamine oxidase activity in human alchoholics. *Medical Biology*, **55**, 181–186.

Ziegler, V. E., Clayton, P. J., Taylor, J. R., Co, B. T., and Biggs, J. T. (1976) Nortriptyline plasma levels and clinical response. *Clinical Pharmacology and Therapeutics*, **20**, 458–463.

The Biochemistry of Psychiatric Disturbances
Edited by G. Curzon
© 1980 John Wiley & Sons Ltd.

CHAPTER 2

Biochemical Abnormalities in Depressive Illness: tryptophan and 5-hydroxytryptamine

KEITH WOOD AND ALEC COPPEN

CHARACTERISTICS AND METHODS OF INVESTIGATION OF THE ILLNESS

One of the most important characteristics of a depressive illness is a profound change of affective state with prominent subjective feelings of sadness. We refer the reader to a detailed account of the symptomatology of depression by Hamilton (1978). It is important not to confuse depressive illness with depressed mood provoked by frustration or loss. The fact that we may then become miserable and lose our appetite does not necessarily signify that we are suffering from a depressive illness.

The expectation of developing an affective illness in a lifetime of 75 years is 3.5% in men and 5.8% in women (Slater and Cowie, 1971). These illnesses usually arise in middle and old age with a mean age of onset of 42 years (Angst et al., 1973). Untreated episodes typically last for 6-12 months and then spontaneously remit but commonly recur. Studies of the natural history of the illness suggest that the intervals between episodes progressively diminish.

Two main subdivisions of the syndrome have been defined (i) bipolar illness in which attacks of both mania (elevation of mood) and depression occur and (ii) unipolar illness in which only depressive episodes occur. This chapter will be concerned primarily with the depressive (unipolar) disorders which account for most cases of affective illness.

Early investigations into the biochemistry of depressive illness were stimulated by the observation of the effects of various drugs on mood or behaviour. The structural similarity of the hallucinogenic drug lysergic acid diethylamide and the neurotransmitter 5-hydroxytryptamine (5-HT) led Woolley and Shaw (1954) to propose that 5-HT might be involved in the regulation of mental processes. The anti-hypertensive drug reserpine depletes monoamines (Carlsson et al., 1957) and caused depression in some patients. Conversely, mood elevation occurred in tuberculosis patients treated with iproniazid, a drug which inhibits monoamine oxidase, an enzyme involved in the catabolism of monoamines. The chance observation that certain tricyclic compounds had an antidepressant action was followed by the finding that they inhibited the re-uptake of released monoamines in brain slices and synaptosomal preparations. All these observations stimulated hypotheses of depression (Schildkraut, 1965; Coppen, 1967) postulating absolute or relative deficiencies of various monoamines in the brains of depressive patients.

The importance of genetic factors to the illness has been investigated for many years. Twin studies have shown the high concordance rates for depressive illness in monozygotic twins compared to dizygotic twins of the same sex. Angst (1966) concluded that bipolar illness arose from a major autosomal gene, whereas unipolar illness was multifactorial. If the inherited component is important then biochemical abnormalities of some kind must be involved in the aetiology of these conditions.

Biochemical investigations into depressive illness are difficult for many reasons. Firstly, there can be no really adequate animal models of depression. Secondly, post-mortem studies of depressed suicides have their limitations, as the psychiatric, drug, and nutritional states of the patient are   rarely fully known and terminal states may greatly affect metabolism. Also, intervals between death and storage of tissues at lower temperatures are inevitably variable. These difficulties may be compounded by the fact that many depressive suicides may have been suffering from a form of depression with specific biochemical characteristics (Åsberg et al., 1976). At present, therefore, biochemists must largely be content with the analysis of blood, CSF, and urine from depressed patients.

This chapter is not a comprehensive review of the biochemistry of the affective disorders. The selection of material is based on our own research interests. Before these investigations are presented and discussed it is important to explain how we carry out our research.

Studies on the chemical pathology of depression should, ideally, be initiated during an episode of the illness before the patient is treated with antidepressants (which may well affect the variates under investigation). We therefore ensure that the patient has been drug-free for 7–10 days before biochemical investigation. The tests should be repeated after recovery and again when the patient has discontinued active treatments. The data on these patients are then compared with those of normal subjects (without a history of psychiatric illness) matched for age and sex and tested under the same conditions as the patients. These conditions are difficult to achieve especially because treatments for depression are now widely used so that untreated patients are rarely available.

Two types of biochemical abnormality are potentially detectable:

1. Abnormalities which disappear on clinical recovery.
2. Abnormalities which do not disappear on clinical recovery and may possibly represent a biochemical predisposition to depressive episodes which are then triggered off by other factors.

We have used these methods for our own biochemical investigations into depressive illness in which we have principally studied processes affecting the amount of 5-HT released from presynaptic nerve terminals. These processes crucially influence mon-oamine transmission and include synthesis and transport, compartmentation, intra-neuronal metabolism and re-uptake mechanisms. We have studied some of these areas of presynaptic regulation of 5-HT in depressed patients.

TRYPTOPHAN METABOLISM

5-HT is synthesized from the essential amino acid tryptophan which is present in the plasma in two forms. An equilibrium exists between tryptophan bound to plasma protein and the non-bound or 'free' form (McMenamy and Oncley, 1958). Approximately 10–20% of the total tryptophan in human plasma is present in this free form. Since the rate-limiting enzyme (tryptophan hydroxylase) of 5-HT synthesis is not saturated with tryptophan, the concentration of tryptophan in the brain and the availability of tryptophan from the plasma in the region of the blood–brain barrier are of major importance for 5-HT synthesis. Controversies have developed on whether plasma total or free tryptophan concentration influences brain trypto-phan levels. These issues have recently been discussed in detail (Fernstrom, 1979; Curzon, 1979; see also p. 90).

It is difficult, however, to study this problem directly in man but it may be pos-sible to apply a single circulation multiple tracer diffusion technique that has been used to measure *in vivo* the fractional loss of labelled amino acids from blood into the brain of dogs (Yudilevich *et al.,* 1972). This tracer technique has been applied to the human brain (Lassen *et al*., 1971) and perhaps the mechanisms and kinetics of transport of tryptophan into the human brain may be explored in this way. Another major factor that can influence brain tryptophan concentration is the con-centration in plasma of other neutral amino acids (leucine, isoleucine, valine, tyro-sine, and phenylalanine) which compete with tryptophan for transport into the brain (Fernstrom and Wurtman, 1972).

The synthesis of brain 5-HT is only a minor pathway of tryptophan metabolism as peripheral metabolism accounts for approximately 98% of the total metabolism so that only a small proportion of tryptophan enters the brain. An important extra-cerebral pathway of tryptophan metabolism is initiated by the action on it of the liver enzyme tryptophan pyrrolase. This enzyme can be induced by its own sub-strate (tryptophan) and also by corticosteroids by distinct mechanisms (Knox and Auerbach, 1955). Increased activity of pyrrolase would tend to divert tryptophan from 5-HT formation and also lead to the formation of pyrrolase pathway meta-bolites e.g. kynurenine that may reduce transport of tryptophan into the brain (Green and Curzon, 1970). It may also possibly affect 5-HT receptor interactions, as administration of kynurenine and 3-hydroxykynurenine has marked effects on both 5-HT and 5-hydroxytryptophan (5-HTP)-induced head twitches in mice (Handley and Miskin, 1977).

The clinical efficacy of the administration of tryptophan with or without a monoamine oxidase inhibitor (Coppen *et al.,* 1967) to depressive patients focused attention on tryptophan concentrations in the plasma of depressive patients. Coppen *et al.* (1973) reported that depressed female patients had significantly reduced plasma free tryptophan concentrations when compared to a group of normal female controls. Total, free and bound tryptophan concentrations in a large group of female depressed patients and controls are shown in Table 1. There was no significant difference between the mean plasma total tryptophan concentration of the controls or acutely depressed drug-free patients, but the mean plasma free tryptophan concentration was significantly decreased in the latter group. No relationship could be detected between free plasma tryptophan or percentage free tryptophan and family history, number of previous episodes of depression, severity of the illness or clinical outcome.

Decreased plasma free concentrations of tryptophan have also been reported in depressive patients by Kishimoto and Hama (1976) and Aylward (1973) but Riley and Shaw (1976), Niskanen *et al.* (1976), and Møller *et al.* (1976) did not find low values. It is interesting that Møller *et al.* (1976) found that a small group of patients who responded strikingly to oral tryptophan medication were also characterized by low availability of plasma tryptophan to the brain suggested by low ratios of total plasma tryptophan to competing amino acids.

Possible explanations for the discrepancies in the level of plasma free tryptophan reported by different workers may be grouped under two main headings (i) methodology of tryptophan determination and (ii) classification of patients.

METHODOLOGY OF TRYPTOPHAN DETERMINATION

The free fraction of tryptophan in the plasma of depressed patients was estimated in our experiments by physically separating it from the bound fraction by ultrafiltration at physiological pH with subsequent fluorimetric determination of tryptophan in the ultrafiltrate (Eccleston, 1973). Free tryptophan has also been separated from bound tryptophan using commercial ultrafiltration cones (Amicon centricones) and centrifugation (Knott and Curzon, 1972). Small scale equilibrium dialysis using radio-labelled L-tryptophan as a tracer has also been used to determine plasma free tryptophan (Bender *et al.*, 1975). Total and free plasma tryptophan concentrations have been measured fluorimetrically by using modifications (Eccleston, 1973; Bloxam and Warren, 1974) of the method of Denckla and Dewey (1967). These modifications are based on the choice of reagent for the precipitation procedure i.e. either perchloric acid (PCA) or trichloroacetic acid (TCA).

In an attempt to estimate the extent to which these differences in methodology contribute to the conflicting results on free tryptophan reported by different workers, we have made a comparative study of some of the available methods for the determination of total and free plasma tryptophan (Wood *et al.*, 1977).

The PCA and TCA methods for the determination of plasma total and free tryptophan give values that are highly correlated although concentrations of tryptophan found were considerably lower using TCA. Similarly results obtained

Table 1. Plasma total, free, and bound tryptophan concentrations in female depressive patients and controls. Reproduced from Coppen and Wood (1978) with permission of Cambridge University Press

Group	N	Age (years)	Total	Plasma tryptophan (μmol l^{-1}) Free	Bound	Free as % of total
Control subjects	51	47.7 ± 0.8	58.8 ± 1.47	6.71 ± 0.25	52.0 ± 0.98	11.5 ± 0.4
Depressed patients	50	55.1 ± 1.9	59.8 ± 1.47	4.07* ± 0.20	55.9 ± 1.47	7.1* ± 0.3

*Significantly less than controls; $p < 0.001$
Results as means ± S.E.M.

Table 2. Concentration of plasma free tryptophan in plasma by different methods. Reproduced from Wood *et al.* (1977) with permission of *Clinica Chimica Acta*

Method	N	Plasma free tryptophan (μmol l^{-1}) Ultrafiltration	Equilibrium dialysis
PCA	10	4.02 ± 0.49*	6.13 ± 0.44
TCA	10	8.24 ± 1.08	9.41 ± 0.64

*Significantly lower than PCA-equilibrium dialysis; $p < 0.001$ (paired comparisons)
Results as means ± S.E.M. Correlation between ultrafiltration and equilibrium dialysis (PCA method) r = 0.72; $p < 0.02$. Correlation between ultrafiltration and equilibrium dialysis (TCA method) r = 0.71; $p < 0.05$.

with our ultrafiltration technique correlated significantly with the centricone method though results were rather lower in the latter case. Table 2 illustrates the very different absolute values we obtained using different techniques. The equilibrium dialysis apparatus described by Moe and Hammes (1974) has been modified in our laboratory and is now our routine method for the determination of plasma free tryptophan concentrations since it satisfies several important requirements: (i) it utilizes small (100 μl) sample of plasma; (ii) pH is controlled; and (iii) many (48) samples can be studied simultaneously, e.g. for Scatchard (1949) plot analysis.

In our estimation this technique and the ultrafiltration system described by Bloxam *et al.* (1977) are ideal methods for the estimation of plasma free tryptophan.

PLASMA FREE TRYPTOPHAN AND TYPE OF DEPRESSION

Problems of psychiatric classification of depression make biochemical investigations extremely difficult and may well underly some discrepancies between biochemical findings reported by different groups. In an attempt to explain conflicting reports on plasma free tryptophan in depression we have retrospectively divided our patients into three groups according to their Newcastle scale score (Carney *et al.*, 1965) in which high scores are associated with depression of a predominantly endogenous type. This classification scale has recently been shown (Rao and Coppen, 1979) to have predictive value for the clinical effect of tricyclic antidepressants and electro-convulsive therapy (ECT). Patients with scores $\geqslant 4$ on this scale, i.e., with more endogenous features, were found to respond to ECT and tricyclic drugs, whereas those patients with a score of $\leqslant 3$, i.e. non-endogenous patients with marked anxiety, do not respond well to these treatments. Plasma tryptophan estimations in these groups of patients are shown in Table 3. While there are no significant differences in the levels of plasma free or total tryptophan there is a trend towards lower plasma free typtophan levels in patients with features more characteristic of endogenous depression. This result may explain some of the discrepant plasma free

Table 3. Mean total and free plasma tryptophan concentration from female depressed patients divided into groups according to Newcastle scale score

Group	N	Plasma tryptophan (μmol l^{-1}) Total	Free
0–3	5	59.3 ± 2.94	5.93 ± 0.64
4–8	16	62.7 ± 1.54	5.20 ± 0.49
⩾9	8	62.3 ± 5.25	4.71 ± 0.59

Results as means ± S.E.M.

tryptophan findings by different groups of workers. It may be that the general practitioner now has relatively effective antidepressant treatments at his disposal for more endogenous forms of depression, but not for less endogenous forms of the illness and that patients of the latter kind are contributing more substantially to in-patient research material. This may explain conflicting plasma tryptophan and other biochemical results. It is important to be aware of the subgroups in primary depressive illness when planning research in this area and analysing results. Perhaps further retrospective and prospective studies such as the one presented here but carried out in other centres, would explain conflicting findings. Certainly, according to our own results low levels of free plasma tryptophan do exist in female depressive patients. We have therefore investigated several biochemical influences on tryptophan binding in plasma.

FACTORS AFFECTING TRYPTOPHAN-ALBUMIN BINDING

Almost all the bound tryptophan in plasma is combined with albumin. This binding is weakened by non-esterified fatty acids (Curzon, et al., 1973) and it has been reported that percentage free tryptophan and unesterified fatty acid concentrations correlate significantly in groups of psychiatric and normal subjects (Curzon et al., 1974). The abnormally low levels of free tryptophan in the plasma of depressed patients cannot be accounted for by low concentrations of plasma proteins and in particular albumin (whether measured by the bromocresol green method (Table 4) or by immunodiffusion techniques (Wood, unpublished observations). Unlike Curzon et al. (1974) we have not detected a positive and significant correlation between percentage free tryptophan and non-esterified fatty acid levels. More importantly our results do not suggest that the low plasma free tryptophan concentrations we find in depression are due to low plasma non-esterified fatty acid values (Table 4). On the contrary, the latter are significantly high perhaps as a consequence of stress (Taggart and Carruthers, 1971). This would (if anything) increase rather than decrease free tryptophan concentration.

It is obvious that stress could have an important role in the aetiology of depres-

Table 4. Protein, albumin, and non-esterified fatty acid (NEFA) levels in plasma of control subjects and depressed patients. Reproduced from Wood and Coppen (1978) with permission of *Neuropharmacology*

Group	N	Protein $(g \, dl^{-1})$	Albumin $(g \, dl^{-1})$	NEFA $(mEq \, l^{-1})$
Control subjects	9	7.1 ± 0.20	4.5 ± 0.1	0.42 ± 0.07
Depressed patients	7	7.1 ± 0.04	4.6 ± 0.1	$0.68^* \pm 0.09$

*Significantly higher than control subjects; $p < 0.05$
Results as means $\pm$ S.E.M.

sive illness, especially in its non-endogenous forms. It is of interest that a multi-compartmental analysis of tryptophan metabolism in depressive illness (Shaw *et al.*, 1978) has been interpreted to suggest that depressive patients are unable to maintain normal amounts of tryptophan in the body because of an idiosyncratic response to stress.

One of the most well defined findings in the field of depressive disorders is their relationship with age and sex. The menopause has been implicated as a possible cause or contributory factor in the onset of the illness and we have reported significantly lower levels of plasma free tryptophan during the perimenopausal (47–55 years) period in normal control subjects (Coppen and Wood, 1978). This may be of aetiological significance for depressive illness. As oestrogens displace tryptophan from plasma protein binding *in vitro* (Aylward, 1973) and increase plasma free tryptophan when given to depressive patients (Coppen and Wood, 1978) perhaps the decrease in free tryptophan levels in the perimenopause mirrors the decrease in circulating oestrogens.

The K_{diss} of albumin binding sites can be calculated using equilibrium dialysis methods, and such techniques have been used to measure this in depressive patients and control subjects (Wood and Coppen, 1978). At 4 °C no significant differences could be detected in the mean value of K_{diss} (depressed patients = $54.2 \pm 3.8 \, \mu M^{-1}$; control subjects = $49.7 \pm 5.0 \, \mu M^{-1}$). Recent experiments at 37 °C (Wood, Swade and Coppen, unpublished results) suggest that in some individuals there is also a significant amount of non-specific binding.

We have also investigated the binding of tryptophan to plasma proteins *in vivo* using clofibrate, a drug used in the management of coronary patients which displaces tryptophan from plasma albumin. Both controls and depressed patients have significantly reduced total plasma tryptophan concentrations after three days of treatment with the drug (Table 5). Only the depressed patients, however, had a significantly elevated plasma free tryptophan concentration compared to their baseline values. The fall of total tryptophan in both controls and depressive patients may be attributed to its displacement from binding (Spano *et al.*, 1974) and consequent increased transport into and utilization by the tissues.

Table 5. Mean plasma tryptophan levels in patients and controls before and after clofibrate. Reproduced from Wood and Coppen (1978) with permission of *Neuropharmacology*

| Group | N | Total | Plasma tryptophan (μmol l^{-1}) | | | | |
| | | | Before clofibrate | | Total | After 3 days clofibrate | |
			Free	Bound		Free	Bound
Control subjects	9	64.4 ± 2.5	6.08 ± 0.74	58.3 ± 1.96	42.2‡ ± 3.4	6.42 ± 0.34	35.8‡ ± 3.4
Depressed patients	7	59.8 ± 4.4	3.90 ± 0.29	55.9 ± 4.41	40.8† ± 3.9	5.49* ± 0.34	35.3† ± 3.9

Difference from baseline: *$p < 0.01$; †$p < 0.005$; ‡$p < 0.001$
Results as means ± S.E.M.

This seems to have occurred in the control subjects as the concentration of plasma free tryptophan has remained virtually constant. The increased concentration of plasma free tryptophan in the depressed patients suggests reduced uptake by the tissues. These results appear to substantiate earlier findings of Paoletti *et al.* (1975) who intravenously injected radioactive tryptophan into control subjects and depressed patients. In the control subjects the disappearance of labelled tryptophan was rapid and was accelerated further by clofibrate treatment. The rate of disapperance of labelled tryptophan from the plasma of the depressed patients was very low and was not altered by clofibrate. Somewhat similarly Coppen *et al.* (1974) reported the slower disappearance of tryptophan from the plasma of depressed patients when compared to a control group.

These studies indicated that transport mechanisms for tryptophan may be abnormal during a depressive illness. Consequently, we became interested in looking for a model to study the kinetics of tryptophan accumulation.

TRYPTOPHAN TRANSPORT MECHANISMS

As uptake kinetics of tryptophan by the blood platelets and synaptosomes are similar (Boullin and Green, 1972), we have studied platelet tryptophan uptake in depressed patients and controls (Wood *et al.*, 1979). Results are shown in Table 6. The Michaelis–Menten uptake parameters (K_m and V_{max}) were both increased (albeit not significantly) in drug free, acutely depressed patients and $\bar{y}$ (the mean uptake over the five concentrations of labelled tryptophan used in the experiment) was significantly increased. This evidence of increased accumulation of tryptophan by blood platelets of depressed patients does not seem to obviously support previous data concerning tryptophan transport in depressive illness. It may possibly contribute to the reduced levels of free tryptophan in the plasma of depressed patients. Platelets and perhaps also red blood cells may be important in the regulation of plasma tryptophan.

Rafaelson (1976) has suggested that the red blood cell may be used as a model for the blood–brain barrier even though it is far from ideal. Rafaelson's results suggest that the monoamine oxidase inhibitors iproniazid and nialamide reduce the uptake of L-tryptophan and L-leucine into erythrocytes *in vitro* by interfering with facilitated transport. It would be interesting to see whether these inhibitors also affect our platelet system.

Our interest in the regulation of plasma tryptophan levels by transport mechanisms led us to investigate the kidneys' role in tryptophan metabolism by examining the urinary excretion of tryptophan by depressed patients (Wood *et al.*, 1978b). Urinary concentration and 24 h excretion of tryptophan by controls and depressed patients are shown in Table 7. Normal quantities of tryptophan were excreted by the depressed patients as a whole. However, when the patients were divided into two groups according to their Newcastle scale score, those with a score of $\geqslant 4$ (more endogenous) excreted significantly smaller amounts of tryptophan during a

Table 6. Tryptophan uptake characteristics (K_m, V_{max} and $\bar{y}$) of platelets from controls and depressed patients

Group	N	Age	$K_m (\mu M)$	V_{max}(pmol 10^8 platelets^{-1} min^{-1})	$\bar{y}$(pmol 10^8 platelets^{-1} min^{-1})
Control subjects	22	47.8 ± 2.7	5.0 ± 0.5	40.7 ± 4.7	11.2 ± 1.0
Depressed patients	20	50.9 ± 2.8	7.7 ± 1.3	54.3 ± 6.5	14.9* ± 1.5

*Significantly higher than control subjects, $p < 0.05$
$\bar{y}$ = mean uptake over the five concentrations of labelled tryptophan used
Results as means ± S.E.M.

Table 7. Mean tryptophan concentration and volume of urine collected from controls, depressed patients and depressed patients divided into two groups according to Newcastle rating scale score. Reproduced from Wood et al. (1978b) with permission of Clinica Chimica Acta

Group	N	Age	Urinary tryptophan		Urine volume (ml 24 h^{-1})
			nmol ml^{-1}	μmol 24 h^{-1}	
Controls	19	49.6 ± 1.9	37.1 ± 4.0	41.5* ± 2.7	1201 ± 60
All depressed patients	20	53.6 ± 3.2	37.9 ± 5.1	37.1 ± 3.2	1251 ± 170
Depressed patients Newcastle score $\leqslant 3$	8	50.9 ± 5.5	44.4 ± 7.0	47.9† ± 4.6	1196 ± 151
Depressed patients Newcastle score $\geqslant 4$	12	55.4 ± 3.9	33.6 ± 7.1	29.8 ± 2.8	1287 ± 260

*Significantly higher than depressed patients with Newcastle score $\geqslant 4$, $p < 0.01$
†Significantly higher than depressed patients with Newcastle score $\geqslant 4$, $p < 0.005$
Results as means ± S.E.M.

Table 8. Correlation coefficients (r) of plasma (total, bound, free, and percentage free) tryptophan and urinary tryptophan of controls. Reproduced from Wood *et al.* (1978b) with permission of *Clinica Chimica Acta*

Plasma tryptophan	N	Urinary tryptophan nmol ml^{-1}	μmol 24 h^{-1}
Total	9	0.41	0.55
Bound	7	0.60	0.88*
% Free	8	−0.64	−0.85*
Free	7	−0.63	−0.76†

*$p < 0.01$; †$p < 0.05$

24 h period when compared to depressed patients with Newcastle scale score $\leqslant 3$, and the control group. These differences could not be accounted for by variations in 24 h urine volumes.

The relationships between plasma and urine tryptophan concentrations in a group of affectively normal, female controls are shown in Table 8. The significant negative correlation between plasma free tryptophan and urinary tryptophan output is an intriguing finding.

The low 24 h urinary tryptophan output from the patients with endogenous features of depression is not accompanied by the elevated plasma free tryptophan levels that might be expected from the correlations between urine and plasma tryptophan levels. Paradoxically, the depressed patients have both low plasma free tryptophan levels and low 24 h urinary tryptophan output. Controlling mechanisms for tryptophan metabolism in the kidney may therefore be abnormal in depressed patients.

TRYPTOPHAN PYRROLASE AND DEPRESSIVE ILLNESS

The liver plays an important part in tryptophan metabolism (Bloxam *et al.*, 1974) and the possible significance of this in depression has been the subject of much interest in recent years.

Curzon and Bridges (1970) reported that female depressed patients excrete significantly more kynurenine than female controls after L-tryptophan loads which suggests that the activity of hepatic tryptophan pyrrolase may be increased during a depressive illness. Since the enzyme accounts for most of tryptophan metabolism it has been suggested that diversion of tryptophan along this pathway may reduce the amounts available for 5-HT synthesis. Although there is a direct correlation between pyrrolase activity in liver biopsy samples *in vitro* and urinary kynurenine levels (Altman and Greengard, 1966), the urinary excretion may be complicated by renal factors. The introduction of a sensitive, specific method for the determination

Table 9. Plasma kynurenine concentrations of controls and depressed patients. Reproduced from Wood *et al.* (1978a) with permission of *Psychopharmacology*

Group	N	Age	Plasma kynurenine (nmol ml^{-1})
Male controls	14	53.1 ± 2.91	2.33 ± 0.12
Female controls	16	52.5 ± 2.14	2.35 ± 0.12
Male depressed patients	10	55.9 ± 4.82	2.40 ± 0.19
Female depressed patients	17	59.6 ± 2.36	2.25 ± 0.14

Results as means ± S.E.M.

of kynurenine in plasma (Joseph and Risby, 1975) has facilitated the measurement of plasma kynurenine in depressed patients without the artificial conditions of a tryptophan load (Wood *et al.*, 1978a). We find that there are no significant differences between depressed patients and controls (Table 9) and that plasma kynurenine concentrations of the former group do not change on recovery. These results, together with those of Møller *et al.*, (1976) suggest that pyrrolase activity is not significantly increased during a depressive illness. This is perhaps surprising as the induction of tryptophan pyrrolase by cortisol (Thomson and Mikuta, 1954) which has been reported to be elevated in depressive illness (Sachar *et al.*, 1973) might be expected to increase the plasma concentrations of kynurenine. The reduced concentration of plasma free tryptophan in depressive illness may, however, obscure any such induction by cortisol. The presence of kynurenine in rat brain (Joseph, 1977) and evidence for a brain enzyme with pyrrolase activity (Gal, 1974) suggests the possibility of interaction between 5-HT and pyrrolase pathway metabolites such as kynurenine in the brain. Pharmacological evidence suggests that this can occur (Gould and Handley, 1978). Therefore it is conceivable that kynurenine has some physiological role in the regulation of tryptophan and 5-HT pathways within the central nervous system.

It has been suggested that either allopurinol or nicotinic acid derivatives may enhance the antidepressant effects of tryptophan by inhibiting its destruction by hepatic tryptophan pyrrolase and thus increasing its availability to the brain (Young and Sourkes, 1974; Badawy and Evans, 1974). Recently, Chouinard *et al.* (1978) have found that a tryptophan–nicotinamide–imipramine combination is superior to either tryptophan plus nicotinamide or imipramine in the treatment of depression. It will be interesting to see whether these manipulations can be used in the treatment of depression.

5-HT METABOLISM

5-HT and other transmitters released from presynaptic terminals within the central nervous system can act on postsynaptic receptors. They are removed from these principally by energy-dependent re-uptake processes which are inhibited by tricyclic antidepressants. We have therefore become increasingly interested in this re-uptake process in depressive illness. However, as it is difficult to investigate in the human central nervous system we have studied blood platelets which share many morphological and biochemical characteristics with the central nervous system serotoninergic synaptosomes. (Sneddon, 1973; Stahl, 1977). Furthermore, the presence of α-adrenoreceptors (Kafka et al., 1977; Newman et al., 1978) and 5-HT receptors on rat (Drummond and Gordon 1975), and human platelets (Boullin et al., 1977) encourages work on the platelet as a model of abnormalities in depressive illness.

Kinetic analysis using low substrate concentrations and measuring the initial uptake rate have shown that the uptake of 5-HT into the platelets of depressed patients is decreased (Tuomisto and Tukiainen, 1976). Our data (Coppen et al., 1978b) confirms these findings (Table 10). The Michaelis constant (K_m) is essentially identical in drug-free depressive patients and control subjects. The transport rate of 5-HT through the platelet membrane (V_{max}) however, is significantly lower in depressive patients. These results suggest that the binding of 5-HT to platelet membrance binding sites is normal in depressed patients but that transport of 5-HT through the platelet membrane is impaired. These changes may be secondary and possibly compensatory to depression but in view of evidence for their persistence after clinical recovery (Table 10) this is unlikely.

The transport of 5-HT into platelets is an active process coupled to a Na^+/K^+ adenosine triphosphatase (ATPase) and depends on Na^+ concentration. The activity of this enzyme in erythrocyte membranes of depressed patients is significantly reduced (Hesketh et al., 1977) but apparently not in platelets (Scott and Reading, 1978). These authors suggest that the platelet preparation used in the study was a heterogeneous mixture of membranes of mitochondrial, granule–membrane, endoplasmic–reticulum, and plasma membrane origin. Thus assay of the enzyme activity in pure preparations of platelet plasma membranes might detect differences similar to those found in erythrocytes. Reduced activity of Na^+/K^+ ATPase in plasma membrane of blood platelets would lead to elevated intracellular levels of Na^+ and diminished intracellular 5-HT levels which have been reported to occur in depression (Coppen 1967, Coppen et al., 1976). Further studies of this enzyme system in depressive illness are therefore warranted.

Amitriptyline, a tricyclic antidepressant drug, competitively inhibits 5-HT transport into the platelets of depressed patients after four weeks of treatment (Table 11). The increased K_m correlates significantly with plasma concentrations of amitriptyline (but not nortriptyline; Table 12).

The lack of correlation between the re-uptake inhibition and clinical improvement is striking (Table 13). These results then cast doubt on the common assumption that these drugs owe their antidepressant effect to re-uptake inhibition. Indeed mianserin, an effective antidepressant, significantly increases the value of V_{max} of platelet 5-HT transport towards control values in depressed patients (Table 14). Mianserin also (in common with amitriptyline and nortriptyline) blocks postsynap-

Table 10. 5-HT uptake (K_m and V_{max}) of platelets from depressed patients and control subjects. Reproduced from Coppen et al. (1978a) with permission of *Clinica Chimica Acta*

Group	N	Age (years)	K_m (μM)	V_{max} (pmol 10^8 platelets^{-1} min^{-1})
Study 1				
Control subjects	20	53.4 ± 1.8	0.54 ± 0.04	25.81 ± 2.19
Acutely depressed patients	13	57.1 ± 3.0	0.53 ± 0.06	18.22 ± 1.75*
Study 2				
Acutely depressed patients	8	58.3 ± 2.9	0.52 ± 0.07	17.40 ± 2.41
Recovered depressed patients	8	58.3 ± 2.9	0.55 ± 0.07	16.25 ± 2.86

*Significantly lower than controls: $p < 0.02$
Results as means ± S.E.M.

Table 11. Platelet 5-HT uptake characteristics (K_m and V_{max}) from 14 patients treated with amitryptyline

Uptake characteristic		Amitriptyline
K_m (μM)	Baseline	0.60 ± 0.09
	4 weeks	2.65* ± 0.64
V_{max} (pmol) 10^8 platelets^{-1} min^{-1})	Baseline	21.4 ± 2.5
	4 weeks	27.3 ± 2.7

*Significantly different from baseline, $p < 0.01$
Results as means ± S.E.M.

Table 12. Correlation coefficients (r) between 5-HT uptake characteristics after four weeks treatment with amitriptyline and plasma drug levels in 11 patients

Uptake characteristic	Amitriptyline	Nortriptyline	Amitriptyline + nortriptyline
4 week K_m	0.67*	0.53	0.67*
ΔK_m	0.77†	0.53	0.69*
% change in K_m	0.80†	0.58	0.74*

*$p < 0.05$; †$p < 0.01$

Table 13. Correlation coefficients (r) between platelet 5-HT uptake characteristics (K_m and V_{max}) and clinical change (expressed by the Hamilton Rating Scale, HRS) in 14 patients during treatment with amitriptyline

	6 weeks HRS score	Clinical assessment % Improvement on HRS	Amelioration score
K_m			
4 weeks	0.01	0.07	−0.18
change	0.04	0.10	−0.21
% change	−0.48	0.05	−0.16
V_{max}			
4 weeks	−0.05	0.05	−0.10
change	−0.25	0.21	−0.23
% change	−0.35	0.35	−0.40

Table 14. 5-HT characteristics (K_m and V_{max}) of platelets from control subjects and patients before and during mianserin therapy. Reproduced from Coppen et al. (1978a) with permission of Brit. J. Clin. Pharmac.

	N	Age	$K_m(\mu M)$	V_{max} (pmol 10^8 platelets^{-1} min^{-1})
Control subjects	10	56.1 ± 2.4	0.57 ± 0.04	28.0 ± 3.02
Baseline patients	7	58.0 ± 4.4	0.47 ± 0.04	13.0 ± 1.42†
Patients receiving mianserin	7	58.0 ± 4.4	0.57 ± 0.04*	20.4 ± 4.32‡

*Significantly higher than baseline patients, $p < 0.05$
†Significantly lower than control group, $p < 0.01$
‡Significantly higher than baseline patients, $p < 0.02$
Results as means ± S.E.M.

tic 5-HT receptors (Fuxe *et al.*, 1977) and this perhaps is involved in its antidepressant actions.

Although platelet 5-HT uptake inhibition is a peripheral and not a central effect it is reasonable to use platelets as a model for serotonergic synaptosomes. Thus, the order of activity of tricyclic drugs in blocking 5-HT uptake in human platelet-rich plasma is similar to their activity in blocking 5-HT uptake in the central nervous system (Todrick and Tait, 1969). However, we doubt whether the therapeutic action of these tricyclic drugs is related to their specificity or potency as blockers of 5-HT uptake. Our present investigations are paralleled by previous findings of a lack of correlation between clinical improvement and the inhibition of re-uptake of NA as measured by the tyramine–dose/pressor–response test (Ghose and Coppen, 1977). Hopefully these findings will provoke further investigations on the mode of therapeutic action of tricyclic antidepressants and other physical treatments such as electroconvulsive therapy in depressed patients.

CONCLUSION

We have found that plasma free tryptophan concentrations are low in endogenously depressed patients. Abnormal transport mechanisms for tryptophan may also be present. Discrepant findings in other studies may reflect selection of patients with depressions of different types. Ultimately, we may be able to identify different kinds of depression by biochemical as well as by psychiatric characteristics and responses to treatment.

Our platelet model of central 5-HT containing synaptosomes suggests that the transport of 5-HT like tryptophan, is abnormal in depression but the lack of correlation between therapeutic outcome with tricyclic drugs and the inhibition of re-uptake of NA and 5-HT questions conventional ideas on how these drugs act.

ACKNOWLEDGEMENTS

This work was supported in part by the Medical Research Council. We are indebted to our colleagues, Mrs C. Swade, Mrs J. Harwood, Miss M. Bishop, Mrs M. Metcalfe, Mr J. Bailey, and Dr V. A. Rao for their assistance during our investigations.

REFERENCES

Altman, K., and Greengard, O. (1966) Correlation of kynurenine excretion with lower tryptophan pyrrolase levels in disease and after hydrocortisone induction. *J. Clin. Invest.*, **45**, 1527–1534.

Angst, J. (1966) *Zur Atiologie und Nosologie endogener depressiver psychosen.* Springer, Heidelberg.

Angst, J., Baastrup, P., Grof, P., Hippius, H., Pöldinger, W., and Weis, P. (1973) The course of monopolar depression and bipolar psychosis. *Folia Psychiat. Neurol. Neurochir. Neerl.*, **76**, 489–500.

Åsberg, M., Thorén, P., Träskman, L., Bertilsson, L., and Ringleerger, N. (1976) Serotonin depression—a biochemical subgroup within the affective disorders. *Science*, **191**, 478–480.

Aylward, M. (1973) Plasma tryptophan levels and mental depression in postmenopausal subjects: effects of oral piperazine-oestrone sulphate. *IRCS Med. Sci.*, **1**, 30.

Badawy, A. A. B., and Evans, M. (1974) Tryptophan plus a pyrrolase inhibitor for depression? *Lancet.*, ii, 1209–1210.

Bender, D. A., Boulton, A. P., and Coulson, W. F. (1975) A simple method for the study of tryptophan binding to serum albumin by small-scale equilibrium dialysis: application to animal and human studies. *Biochem. Soc. Trans.*, **3**, 193–194.

Bloxam, D. L., and Warren, W. H. (1974) Error in the determination of tryptophan by the method of Denkla and Dewey. A revised procedure. *Analyt. Biochem.*, **60**, 621–625.

Bloxam, D. L., Warren, W. H., and White, P. J. (1974) Involvement of the liver in the regulation of tryptophan availability. Possible role in the responses of liver and brain to starvation. *Life Sci.*, **15**, 1443–1455.

Bloxam, D. L., Hutson, P. H., and Curzon, G. (1977) A simple apparatus for ultrafiltration of small volumes: application to the measurement of free and albuminbound tryptophan in plasma. *Analyt. Biochem.*, **83**, 130–142.

Boullin, D. J., and Green, A. R. (1972) Mechanisms by which human blood platelets accumulate glycine, GABA, and amino acid precursors of putative neurotransmitters. *Brit. J. Pharmac.*, **45**, 83–94.

Boullin, D. J., Glenton, P. A. M., Molyneux, D., Peters, J. R., and Roach, B. (1977) Binding of 5-hydroxytryptamine to human blood platelets. *Proc. Brit. Pharm. Soc.*, **1977**, 453.

Carlsson, A., Rosengren, E., Bertler, A., and Nilsson, J. (1957) Effect of reserpine on the metabolism of catecholamines, in Garattini, S., and Ghetti, V. (eds.) *Psychotropic Drugs*, Elsevier, Amsterdam, p. 363.

Carney, M. W. P., Roth, M., and Garside, R. F. (1965) The diagnosis of depressive symptoms and the prediction of ECT responses. *Brit. J. Psychiat.*, **111**, 659–674.

Chouinard, G., Young, S., Annable, L., and Sourkes, T. L. (1978) A double-blind controlled study of tryptophan, nicotinamide, imipramine and their combination in depressed patients. *11th C.I.N.P. Congress, Vienna, July, 9-14,* abstracts, p. 319.

Coppen, A. (1967) The biochemistry of the affective disorders. *Brit. J. Psychiat.*, **113**, 1237–1264.

Coppen, A., and Wood, K. (1978) Tryptophan and depressive illness. *Psychol. Med.*, **8**, 49–57.

Coppen, A., Shaw, D. M., Herzberg, B., and Maggs, R. (1967) Tryptophan in the treatment of depression. *Lancet*, ii, 1178–1180.

Coppen, A., Eccleston, E., and Peet, M. (1973) Total and free tryptophan concentration in the plasma of depressive patients. *Lancet*, ii, 60–63.

Coppen, A., Brooksbank, B. W. L., Eccleston, E., Peet, M., and White, S. G. (1974) Tryptophan metabolism in depressive illness. *Psychol. Med.*, **4**, 164–173.

Coppen, A., Turner, P., Rowsell, A. R., and Padgham, C. (1976) 5-Hydroxytryptamine (5-HT) in the whole-blood of patients with depressive illness. *Postgrad. Med. J.*, **52**, 156–158.

Coppen, A., Ghose, K., Swade, C., and Wood, K. (1978a) Effect of mianserin hydrochloride on peripheral uptake mechanisms for noradrenaline and 5-hydroxytryptamine in man. *Br. J. Clin. Pharmac.*, **5**, 13S–17S.

Coppen, A., Swade, C., and Wood, K. (1978b) Platelet 5-hydroxytryptamine accumulation in depressive illness. *Clin. Chim. Acta*, **87**, 165–168.

Curzon, G. (1979) Relationships between plasma, CSF and brain tryptophan. *J. Neural. Trans.*, **suppl. 15**, 81–92.

Curzon, G., and Bridges, P. K. (1970) Tryptophan metabolism in depression. *J. Neurol. Neurosurg. Psychiat.*, **33**, 698–704.

Curzon, G., Friedel, J., and Knott, P. J. (1973) The effect of fatty acids on the binding of tryptophan to plasma protein. *Nature*, **242**, 198–200.

Curzon, G., Friedel, J., Katamaneni, B. D., Greenwood, M. H., and Lader, M. H. (1974) Unesterified fatty acids and the binding of tryptophan in human plasma. *Clin. Sci. Mol. Med.*, **47**, 415–424.

Denckla, W. D., and Dewey, H. K. (1967) The determination of tryptophan in plasma, liver, and urine. *J. Lab. Clin. Invest.*, **69**, 160–169.

Drummond, A. H., and Gordon, J. L. (1975) Specific binding sites for 5-hydroxytryptamine on rat blood platelets. *Biochem. J.*, **150**, 129–132.

Eccleston, E. G. (1973) A method for the estimation of free and total acid-soluble plasma tryptophan using an ultrafiltration technique. *Clin. Chim. Acta*, **48**, 269–272.

Fernstrom, J. D. (1979) Diet induced changes in plasma amino acid pattern: effects on the brain uptake of large neutral amino acids and on brain serotonin synthesis. *J. Neural Trans.*, **suppl. 15**, 55–67.

Fernstrom, J. D., and Wurtman, R. J. (1972) Brain serotonin content: physiological regulation by plasma neutral amino acids. *Science*, **178**, 414–416.

Fuxe, K., Ögren, S-O., Agnati, L., Gustafsson, J. Å., and Jonsson, G. (1977) On the mechanism of action of the antidepressant drugs amitriptyline and nortriptyline. Evidence for 5-hydroxytryptamine receptor blocking activity. *Neuroscience Letters*, **6**, 339–343.

Gal, E. M. (1974) Cerebral tryptophan-2,3-dioxygenase (pyrrolase) and its induction in rat brain. *J. Neurochem.*, **22**, 861–863.

Ghose, K., and Coppen, A. (1977) Noradrenaline, depressive illness and the action of amitriptyline. *Psychopharmacol.*, **54**, 57–60.

Gould, S. E., and Handley, S. L. (1978) Dose-dependent dual action of kynurenine, a tryptophan metabolite, in the turnover of 5-hydroxytryptamine. *Proc. Brit. J. Pharmacol.*, **1978**, 55.

Green, A. R., and Curzon, G. (1970) The effect of tryptophan metabolites on brain 5-hydroxytryptamine metabolism. *Biochem. Pharmacol.*, **19**, 2061–2068.

Hamilton, M. (1978) Mania and depression: classification, description and course, in Paykel, E. S., and Coppen, A. (eds.) *Psychopharmacology of Affective Disorders*, Oxford University Press, Oxford, pp. 1–13.

Handley, S. L., and Miskin, R. C. (1977) The interaction of some kynurenine pathway metabolites with 5-hydroxytryptophan and 5-hydroxytryptamine. *Psychopharmacol.*, **51**, 305–309.

Hesketh, J. E., Glen, A. I. M., and Reading, H. W. (1977) Membrane ATPase activities in depressive illness. *J. Neurochem.*, **28**, 1401–1402.

Joseph, M. H. (1977) The determination of kynurenine by gas-liquid chromatography; evidence for its presence in rat brain. *Brit. J. Pharmacol.*, **59**, 525.

Joseph, M. H., and Risby, D. (1975) The determination of kynurenine in plasma. *Clin. Chim. Acta*, **63**, 197–204.

Kafka, M. S., Tallman, J. F., Smith, C. C., and Costa, J. L. (1977) Alpha-adrenergic receptors on human platelets. *Life Sci.*, **21**, 1429–1438.

Kishimoto, M., and Hama, Y. (1976) The level and diurnal rhythm of plasma tryptophan and tyrosine in manic-depressive patients. *Yokohama Med. Bull.*, **27**, 89–97.

Knott, P. J., and Curzon, G. (1972) Free tryptophan in plasma and brain tryptophan metabolism. *Nature*, **239**, 452–453.

Knox, W. E., and Auerbach, V. H. (1955) The hormonal control of tryptophan peroxidase in rat. *J. Biol. Chem.*, **214**, 307–313.

Lassen, N. A., Trap-Jensen, J., Alexander, S. C., Olesen, J., and Paulson, O. B. (1971). Blood–brain barrier studies in man using the double indicator method. *Amer. J. Physiol.*, **220**, 1627–1633.

McMenamy, R. H., and Oncley, J. L. (1958) The specific binding of L-tryptophan to serum albumin. *J. Biol. Chem.*, **233**, 1436–1447.

Moe, O. A., and Hammes, G. G. (1974) A study of the binding of thiamine diphosphate and thiochrome diphosphate to the pyruvate dehydrogenase multi-enzyme complex. *Biochem.*, **13**, 2547–2552.

Møller, S. E., Kirk, L., and Fremming, K. H. (1976) Plasma amino acids as an index for subgroups in manic depressive psychosis: correlation to effect of tryptophan. *Psychopharmacol.*, **49**, 205–213.

Newman, K. D., Williams, L. T., Bishopric, N. H., and Lefkowitz, R. J. (1978) Identification of α-adrenergic receptors in human platelets by [^{3}H]dihydro-ergocryptine binding. *J. Clin. Invest.*, **61**, 395–402.

Niskanen, P., Huttunen, M., Tamminen, T., and Jääskeläinen, J. (1976) The daily rhythm of plasma tryptophan and tyrosine in depression. *Brit. J. Psychiat.*, **128**, 67–73.

Paoletti, R., Sirtori, C., and Spano, P. F. (1975) Clinical relevance of drugs affecting tryptophan transport. *Ann. Rev. Pharmacol.*, **15**, 73–81.

Rafaelsen, O. (1976) In *Monoamine Oxidase and its Inhibition*. CIBA Foundation Symposium 39 (new series), Elsevier, Amsterdam, p. 294.

Rao, V. A. R., and Coppen, A. (1979) Classification of depression, and response to amitriptyline therapy. *Psychol. Med.*, **9**, 321–325.

Riley, G. J., and Shaw, D. M. (1976) Total and non-bound tryptophan in unipolar illness. *Lancet*, **ii**, 1249.

Sachar, E. J., Hellman, L., Roffwarg, H. P., Halpern, F. S., Fukushima, D. K., and Gallagher, T. F. (1973) Disrupted 24-hour pattern of cortisol secretion in psychotic depression. *Arch. Gen. Psychiat.*, **28**, 19–24.

Scatchard, G. (1949) The attractions of proteins for small molecules and ions. *Ann. N.Y. Acad. Sci.*, **51**, 660–672.

Schildkraut, J. J. (1965) The catecholamine hypothesis of affective disorders: a review of supporting evidence. *Am. J. Psychiat.*, **122**, 509–522.

Scott, M., and Reading, H. W. (1978) A comparison of platelet membrane and erythrocyte membrane adenosine triphosphatase specific activities in affective disorders. *Biochem. Soc. Trans.*, **6**, 642–644.

Shaw, D. M., Tidmarsh, S. F., Johnson, A. L., Michalakeas, A. C., Riley, G. J., Blazek, R., and Francis, A. F. (1978) Multicompartmental analyses of amino acids: II. Tryptophan in affective disorders. *Psychol. Med.*, **8**, 487–494.

Slater, E., and Cowie, V. (1971) Affective psychoses in, *The Genetics of Mental Disorders*, Oxford University Press, London, pp. 72–91.

Sneddon, J. M. (1973) Blood platelets as a model for monoamine-containing neurones. *Prog. Neurobiol.*, **1**, 151–198.

Spano, P. F., Szyszka, K., Galli, C. L., and Ricci, A. (1974) Effect of clofibrate on free and total tryptophan in serum and brain tryptophan metabolism. *Pharmac. Res. Commun.*, **6**, 163–173.

Stahl, S. M. (1977) The human platelet. A diagnostic and research tool for the study of biogenic amines in psychiatric and neurologic disorders. *Arch. Gen. Psychiat.*, **34**, 509–516.

Taggart, P., and Carruthers, M. (1971) Endogenous hyperlipidaemia induced by emotional stress of racing driving. *Lancet*, **i**, 363–366.

Thomson, J. F., and Mikuta, E. T. (1954) The effect of cortisone and hydrocortisone in the tryptophan peroxidase-oxidase activity of rat liver. *Endocrinol.*, **55**, 232–233.

Todrick, A., and Tait, A. C. (1969) The inhibition of human platelet 5-hydroxytryptamine uptake by tricylic antidepressive drugs. The relation between structure and potency. *J. Pharm. Pharmac.*, **21**, 751–762.

Tuomisto, J., and Tukiainen, E. (1976) Decreased uptake of 5-hydroxytryptamine in blood platelets from depressed patients. *Nature*, **262**, 596–598.

Wood, K., and Coppen, A. (1978) The effect of clofibrate on total and free plasma tryptophan in depressed patients. *Neuropharmacol.*, **17**, 417–431.

Wood, K., Swade, C., Harwood, J., Eccleston, E., Bishop, M., and Coppen, A., (1977). Comparison of methods for the determination of total and free tryptophan in plasma. *Clin. Chim. Acta*, **80**, 299–303.

Wood, K., Harwood, J., and Coppen, A. (1978a) The effect of antidepressant drugs on plasma knyurenine in depressed patients. *Psychopharmacol.*, **59**, 263–266.

Wood, K., Harwood, J., Swade, C., and Coppen, A. (1978b) Decreased tryptophan excretion by depressive patients. *Clin. Chim. Acta*, **88**, 57–61.

Wood, K., Swade, C., and Coppen, A. (1979) Tryptophan accumulation by blood platelets of depressed patients. *J. Neural. Trans.*, Suppl. **15**, 161–164.

Woolley, D. W., and Shaw, E. (1954) Some neurophysiological aspects of serotonin. *Brit. Med. J.*, **ii**, 122–127.

Young, S. N., and Sourkes, T. L. (1974) The antidepressant action of tryptophan. *Lancet*, **ii**, 897–898.

Yudilevich, D. L., De Rose, N., and Sepúlveda, F. V. (1972) Facilitated transport of amino acids through the blood–brain barrier of the dog studied in a single capillary circulation. *Brain Res.*, **44**, 569–578.

CHAPTER 3

Changes in Monoamine Function in Rats after Electroconvulsive Shocks: Possible Mechanisms Involved and their Relevance to ECT

A. RICHARD GREEN

INTRODUCTION

Two major approaches are used in the investigation of the biochemical changes which may occur in depressive illness. One involves the examination of biochemical changes occurring in blood, cerebrospinal fluid, urine, platelets, and post-mortem brain tissue. The other approach is to study how drugs, effective in treating depression, alter the biochemistry and function of the brains of experimental animals and then extrapolating from these results to predict biochemical abnormalities associated with depression. Clearly this approach has the inherent problem of deciding which biochemical changes produced by the drug are related to its therapeutic action (e.g. see the review by Green and Costain, 1978).

While much effort has been expended in trying to clarify the antidepressant mechanism of action of various drugs, little attention has been paid to another important but non-pharmacological treatment of severe depression—ECT. It is not the purpose of this chapter to enter into the current controversy surrounding ECT and its efficacy. Several recent papers and reviews have emphasized the safety and efficacy of ECT in severe depression (Royal College of Psychiatrists, 1977; Turek and Hanlon, 1977; *Drug Ther. Bull.*, 1977; Avery and Winokur, 1977). In this chapter I shall discuss only its possible mechanism of action.

METHODS

Behavioural models

Rats were used in all studies. 5-HT function was assessed by measurement of the hyperactivity which follows administration of tranylcypromine and L-tryptophan

Table 1. Scoring system used for catalepsy

Total time of catalepsy (s)	Score
0–10	0
11–30	0.5
31–60	1
61–90	1.5
91–120	2
121–150	2.5
151–180	3
181–210	3.5
211–240	4
241–∞	5

using three rats per cage and LKB Animex meters. Postsynaptic changes were examined by measurement of the hyperactivity which follows injection of the 5-HT agonists 5-methoxy N,N-dimethyltryptamine or quipazine. This approach has been described in detail elsewhere (Green and Grahame-Smith, 1976, 1978).

DA function was examined by measurement of the hyperactivity changes on administration of tranylcypromine and L-Dopa (Green and Kelly, 1976) or the increase in locomotor activity following injection of the DA releasing drug methamphetamine or the agonist apomorphine or measurement of the circling behaviour on administration of either of these drugs to unilaterally nigro-striatal lesioned rats (Ungerstedt, 1971).

Catalepsy was measured in animals following haloperidol (1.5 mg kg^{-1}) by draping the forelimbs over a bar 8 cm high, determining how long they remained in this position and scoring using the scale shown in Table 1.

Biochemical studies

Details of the measurement of rat brain 5-HT, tryptophan, and DA sensitive adenylate cyclase are given in Evans et al. (1976) and Green et al. (1977). GABA turnover was determined using mass fragmentography according to the methods of Bertillson and Costa (1976) and Bertillson et al. (1977).

Electroconvulsive shock administration

ECS was delivered through earclip electrodes from either an Edison portable ECS unit or a Theratronics small animal electroplexy unit. The shock was normally 50 Hz sinusoidal, 150 V for 1 s given to rats lightly anaesthetized with halothane, control rats receiving halothane only.

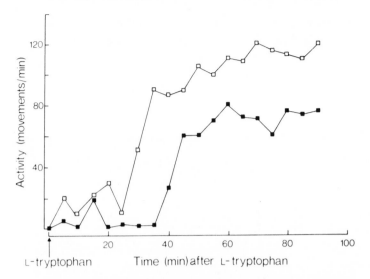

Figure 1. Effect of repeated ECS on hyperactivity following tranylcypromine and L-tryptophan. Rats were given a single ECS each day for ten days. Some 24 h after the final shock they were injected with tranylcypromine (20 mg kg^{-1}, i.p.) and L-tryptophan (50 mg kg^{-1}, i.p.) 30 min later and hyperactivity measured. Control (halothane anaesthesia only) group (■), ECS group (□). For experimental details see Methods section. Reproduced with permission from *British Journal of Pharmacology*

ALTERATION OF MONOAMINE-MEDIATED RESPONSES FOLLOWING ECS

Following a single ECS there was no alteration in the hyperactivity response to tranylcypromine/L-tryptophan, suggesting that there was no alteration in central 5-HT function. However, following a single ECS daily for ten days the rats showed enhanced behavioural responses to tranylcypromine/L-tryptophan administration compared to the control (halothane anaesthetic group) 24 h after the final shock (Figure 1). The rate of brain 5-HT synthesis was the same in both groups of animals suggesting that the altered response was due to some postsynaptic change. This was confirmed by the observation that the responses to the 5-HT agonists, 5-methoxy N,N,-dimethyltryptamine and quipazine were also enhanced by ECS pretreatment (Evans *et al.*, 1976; Green *et al.*, 1977).

DA-mediated behavioural responses were also enhanced by a daily ECS for ten days. The hyperactivity response to tranylcypromine/L-Dopa was increased considerably, as was the locomotor response to a low dose of methamphetamine (1 mg kg^{-1}) (Evans *et al.*, 1976; Green *et al.*, 1977).

The circling response in unilateral nigro-striatally lesioned rats was enhanced following administration of either methamphetamine or apomorphine (Green *et*

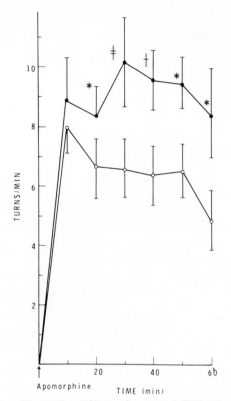

Figure 2. Effect of repeated ECS on the circling behaviour of unilaterally nigrostriatal lesioned rats given apomorphine. Rats were lesioned and given anaesthetic or a single electroconvulsive shock each day for ten days. The figure shows the circling behaviour in turns min^{-1} of the same animals given apomorphine (2 mg kg^{-1}, i.p.) before (●) and two days after the ECS (○). Results as means ± S.E.M. (Seven animals). Statistics calculated by paired t-test. Differences from control values: $*p < 0.01$, $†p < 0.02$, $‡p < 0.05$. Mean turns min^{-1} during 60 min. Control 38.8 ± 5.7, ECS 54.7 ± 6.7, $p < 0.01$. Reproduced with permission from *Psychopharmacology*

al., 1977). The response to the latter drug is particularly interesting as although the turning after apomorphine is considered to result from stimulation of a receptor 'supersensitive' because of the denervation, treatment with ECS caused this 'supersensitive' response to increase further (Figure 2).

All this data, therefore, suggested that repeated ECS in some way increased the behavioural responses that result when central 5-HT and DA function is increased and that the changes were occurring postsynaptically. This view was strengthened by the work of Modigh (1975) who observed that behavioural responses of mice either to apomorphine or to reserpine followed by apomorphine plus clonidine (a procedure thought to increase NAergic function in the brain) were increased following ECS administration for around eight days.

It is generally believed that endogenous depression can be alleviated by drugs which apparently increase monoamine function, e.g. L-tryptophan by increasing 5-HT synthesis, monoamine oxidase inhibitors by inhibiting monoamine degradation and tricyclic antidepressants by inhibiting monoamine re-uptake at the nerve ending (although it is by no means uncertain that this property is responsible for the therapeutic action of the above drugs). All these procedures probably increase the amount of monoamine neurotransmitter in the synaptic cleft. In contrast ECT, according to our own and Modigh's (1975) data, may be acting by increasing, in some way, the size of the postsynaptic monoaminergic response to the same amount of released transmitter.

RELEVANCE OF ENHANCED MONOAMINE-MEDIATED BEHAVIOURAL RESPONSES TO THE THERAPEUTIC MECHANISM OF ECT

If the enhanced monoamine-mediated behavioural responses in rats given ECT are relevant to its clinical mechanism then enhancement should occur after giving ECS in ways that are therapeutically beneficial and should not be seen when the ECS is given in ways that do not result in human mood improvement.

In order to investigate relationships between conditions of ECS administration and behavioural responses, we made use of three conditions which have been suggested to be important for successful ECT (Fink, 1974; Kety, 1974) and applied them to the administration of ECS to rats.

Condition 1

'Clinical improvement is dependent on the number and frequency of seizures. Clinical change evolves gradually, the change being initiated by the ECT and sustained by repeated applications. Multiple ECT in one day is rarely successful' (see Abrams, 1974).

The effect of spacing of electroconvulsive seizures on rat behaviour was therefore investigated (Table 2).

It was found that five ECS spaced out over ten days or eight ECS spaced out over 17 days were as successful as one ECS daily for ten days in producing enhanced responses to tranylcypromine/L-tryptophan. Thus when ECS was given in ways closely resembling ECT (2–3 ECT per week for 2–3 weeks (see Royal College of Psychiatrists, 1977)) then enhanced 5-HT responses were seen. In further agreement

Table 2. Effect of different periods of ECS administration on 5-HT mediated behavioural responses

Treatment	Activity (movements per 90 min) experimental	control	Significance p
8 ECS in 8 h, 150 V sinusoidal, 1 s bilateral			
Test day 3	8,970 ± 675	8,664 ± 834	N.S.
Test day 9	9,569 ± 1,160	9,293 ± 1,249	N.S.
8 ECS over 17 days, 150 V sinusoidal, 1 s bilateral	9,340 ± 470	6,080 ± 930	< 0.01
5 ECS over 10 days, 150 V sinusoidal, 1 s bilateral	9,260 ± 1,197	6,400 ± 779	< 0.025

Values as means ± S.D. of at least three experiments

with Condition 1 it was found that multiple ECS in one day (eight shocks spaced out over 8 h) had no effect on the 5-HT-mediated responses either one, three, or nine days later (Costain *et al.*, 1979).

Condition 2

'The persistent therapeutic effects depend on the changes in the central nervous system which accompany the seizure, not on peripheral components or non-specific effects such as anoxia or stress.'

This contention is supported by the observations that preventing the motor component of the blocking drugs does not alter the therapeutic response (Seager, 1959) but that shortening the cerebral seizure with lidocaine lessens the therapeutic effect (Ottosson, 1960).

In agreement with this we found that giving ECS to animals pretreated with the short-acting depolarizing neuromuscular blocking drug fazadinium ('Fazadon') still produced behavioural enhancement. Also non-specific factors such as anoxia or stress did not enhance 5-HT-mediated behaviour. Thus 20 s of hypoxia daily for ten days or giving a potentially convulsive shock to the feet daily for ten days had no enhancing effect. Similarly, subconvulsive shocks were without enhancing effect (Table 3).

Condition 3

'The method of inducing the seizure is less important than the number and frequency of the induced seizures.'

Thus, it was not necessary for the seizures to be produced electrically. This was

Table 3. Effect of neuromuscular blockade and subconvulsive shock on 5-HT mediated behavioural responses

Treatment	Activity (movements per 90 min)		Significance p
	experimental	control	
5 ECS over 10 days, 150 V sinusoidal, 1 s bilateral	9,260 ± 1,197	6,400 ± 779	< 0.025
As above and Fazadinium	8,408 ± 1,358	5,610 ± 390	< 0.025
10 consecutive days subconvulsive shocks, 70 V sinusoidal 1 s bilateral	6,214 ± 843	6,714 ± 1,036	N.S.
10 consecutive days hypoxia (20 s day^{-1} in N_2)	6,513 ± 1,407	5,605 ± 742	N.S.
10 consecutive days foot shock 150 V biphasic, 1 s	8,042 ± 2,936	8,052 ± 806	N.S.

Values as means ± S.D. of at least three experiments

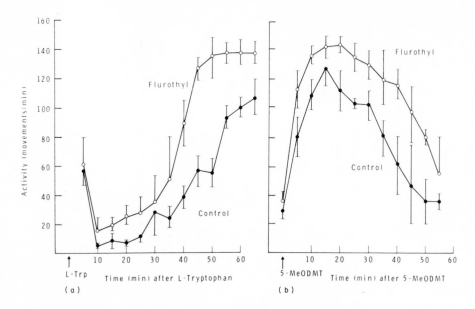

Figure 3.   Hyperactivity response of rats treated with flurothyl to (a) tranylcypro-
mine/L-tryptophan and (b) tranylcypromine/5-methoxy N, N-dimethyltryptamine.
Rats were convulsed daily for ten days by exposure to flurothyl. Some 24 h after
the final convulsion, rats were injected with tranylcypromine (20 mg kg^{-1}) followed
30 min later by either L-tryptophan (L-Tryp) 50 mg kg^{-1} or 5-methoxy N, N-dimethyltryptamine (5-MeODMT) (2 mg kg^{-1}). Means and ranges of three separate
observations (control) and two observations (flurothyl) are shown. Total movements
± S.E.M. during 60 min after L-tryptophan: control, 2,443 ± 267 (3); flurothyl,
4,077 ± 352 (2), $p < 0.025$. Total movements ± S.E.M. during 60 min following 5-
MeODT: control, 4,316 ± 235 (3); flurothyl, 6,327 ± 487 (2), $p < 0.025$. Reproduced with permission from *British Journal of Pharmacology*

shown in experiments in which rats were exposed daily to the inhalant convulsant
agent flurothyl ('Indoklon'; bis (2,2,2, trifluoroethyl) ether, $F_3C.CH_2OCH_2CF_3$)
which has been used successfuly in place of ECT (Krantz *et al.* 1958; Karliner and
Padula, 1959a,b; Fink, *et al.*, 1961; Spreche, 1964). Convulsions occurred and (as
after ECS), behavioural responses to procedures resulting in increased 5-HTergic or
DAergic function were enhanced (Figures 3, 4) (Green, 1978a) It was also found that a
flurothyl convulsion once daily for four days followed by ECS once daily for four
days enhanced DA-mediated responses but that four days on either treatment alone
did not (Figure 4). Alternate treatment with ECT and flurothyl is also said to be
successful clinically (Freund and Warren, 1965).

Other evidence agreeing with Condition 3 is that electrode location, type, and
duration of the current does not effect the therapeutic outcome (Ottosson, 1960;
Valentine *et al.*, 1968; Lancaster *et al.*, 1958). Similarly in our rat work we found

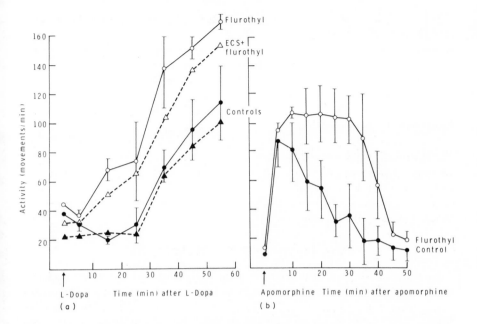

Figure 4.   Hyperactivity response of rats treated with flurothyl to (a) tranylcypro-mine/L-Dopa and (b) apomorphine. Rats were convulsed daily for seven days by exposure to flurothyl. 24 h after the final convulsion rats were injected with (a) tranylcypromine (20 mg kg^{-1}) followed 30 min later by L-Dopa (50 mg kg^{-1}) or (b) apomorphine (2 mg kg^{-1}). Means and ranges of three observations (control) and two observations (flurothyl) are shown. (●) Control (untreated); (○) flurothyl-treated. (△) Response to tranylcypromine and L-Dopa of rats treated for four days with flurothyl followed four days with ECS; (▲) control of this experiment, rats being untreated for four days followed by four days of halothane anaesthesia only. Both groups were given tranylcypromine (20 mg kg^{-1}) followed 30 min later by L-Dopa (50 mg kg^{-1}) 24 h after the final shock. Total movements ± S.E.M. during 60 min following L-Dopa; control, 3,306 ± 428 (3); flurothyl 6,310 ± 630 (2), $p < 0.025$. Total movements ± S.E.M. during 50 min following apomorphine; control, 1,670 ± 569 (3); flurothyl, 4,052 ± 717 (2), $p < 0.05$. Reproduced with permission from *British Journal of Pharmacology*

enhanced responses whether ECS was given via unilaterally or bilaterally placed electrodes and whether the current was sinusoidal or unidirectional (Table 4).

The above groups of experiments show that when procedures found necessary for successful ECT are used in the rat then behavioural responses to 5-HT or DA receptor stimulation are enhanced. Procedures not found to be clinically useful do not alter the behavioural responses (Costain *et al.*, 1979). This work and its rele-vance to ECT has been described in detail (Grahame-Smith *et al.*, 1978; Green, 1978b).

Table 4. Effect of various ECS currents and electrode placements on 5-HT mediated behavioural responses

Treatment	Activity (movements per 90 min) experimental	control	Significance p
10 consecutive days ECS 150 V sinusoidal, 1 s bilateral	10,006 ± 761	6,108 ± 847	< 0.025
10 consecutive days ECS 150 V monophasic, 1 s bilateral	9,587 ± 1,804	6,605 ± 1,546	< 0.05
10 consecutive days ECS 150 V sinusoidal, 1 s unilateral	10,069 ± 1,154	6,422 ± 229	< 0.01

Values as means ± S.D. of at least three experiments

MECHANISM OF THE ENHANCEMENT

An obvious mechanism that would explain the change in behavioural responses would be a change in the characteristics of the receptors mediating them. Such a change occurs for example, in DA receptors on chronic neuroleptic treatment (Burt *et al.*, 1977). However, preliminary data suggest that ECS does not alter [^{3}H]spiroperidol binding in the rat caudate nucleus (C. K. Atterwill, in preparation), Furthermore the activity of DA-sensitive adenylate cyclase (measured *in vitro*) is also unaltered by ECS (Green *et al.*, 1977). It is therefore more probable that alterations in other systems modulating the monoamine-mediated behavioural responses are responsible for their increase.

It may be relevant that several of the monoamine-mediated behavioural changes studied were altered when GABA function in the brain was altered (Green *et al.*, 1976; Cott and Engel 1977). It therefore seemed important to examine the effects of ECS on GABA concentration and turnover in the brain. This was achieved by use of a new mass fragmentographic technique (see Methods section, above). Some 24 h following a single ECS daily for ten days, GABA concentration increased markedly in both the n.accumbens and n.caudatus. No changes were seen in animals 24 h after being given either a single ECS or a sub-convulsive shock daily for ten days (Table 5). Investigation of the rate of GABA synthesis revealed that it was approximately halved in both the n.accumbens and n.caudatus but only in those animals given ECS X 10 (Table 5). No clear changes in either GABA concentration or synthesis rate were seen in the substantia nigra after any treatment.

The raised GABA content and decreased synthesis rate were associated with a decrease in turnover (not shown, see Green *et al.*, 1978). A decrease in synthesis of a transmitter and an increase in its concentration is almost certainly indicative of decreased release. The data thus indicate a probable functional reduction of GABAergic transmission and hence inhibitory tone.

These results suggest that ECS X 10 decreases the inhibitory tone of GABAergic

Table 5. Effect of ECS on GABA concentration and fractional rate constant in brain regions

	N. accumbens		N. caudatus	
	GABA	K_{GABA}	GABA	K_{GABA}
Control	48 ± 4	24 ± 3	25 ± 1	17 ± 1
10 consecutive days ECS 150 V sinusoidal 1 s bilateral	79 ± 10†	12 ± 2*	37 ± 4†	11 ± 1‡
10 consecutive days subconvulsive shocks. As above but 70 V	48 ± 3	26 ± 1	24 ± 2	17 ± 1
1 day ECS 150 V sinusoidal, 1 s bilateral	51 ± 4	27 ± 2	23 ± 2	19 ± 5

Values as means ± S.E.M. of 4–7 determinations. GABA concentration as nmol mg protein^{-1}.
*$p < 0.05$; †$p < 0.01$; ‡$p < 0.001$ compared to control

interneurons in the n.accumbens and n.caudatus. These appear to be postsynaptic to DAergic neurons according to both biochemical (Mao et al., 1977) and behavioural (Green et al., 1977; Cott and Engel, 1977) evidence. This would presumably lead to enhanced DAergic-mediated behaviour as demonstrated for both the n.caudatus (Green et al., 1977) and the n.accumbens (Heal and Green, 1978). As GABA changes were seen in these nuclei but not in the substantia nigra, changes appear to have occurred in interneurons in the former regions but not in the main striato-nigral pathway.

In these experiments met^5-enkephalin content in several brain regions was also determined. Again it was found that only ECS X 10 of all the treatments studied produced changes. These were specific to the n.caudatus, with no change in either the pons-medulla or cortex (Table 6). The 50% increase in met-enkephalin in this region is difficult to interpret in view of the limited data at present available on the significance of changes in the concentration of this peptide. However, if the increased content of this putative transmitter (like that of GABA) indicates decreased release and function it would lead to increased DAergic facilitation, as this peptide modulates DAergic systems in the striatum in an inhibitory fashion via axo-axonic synapses (Pollard et al., 1977).

The question arises: can the postulated change in GABA function be demonstrated behaviourally? This has now been attempted using neuroleptic induced catalepsy as a behavioural model. It is known that amino-oxyacetic acid, which increases GABA concentrations in the brain enhances the cataleptic response of rats to haloperidol (Keller et al., 1976; Worms and Lloyd, 1978). Similarly, the putative GABA-, mimetic drugs muscimol (Naik et al., 1976), benzodiazepines (Costa, 1977; Haefely et al., 1975), and baclofen all increase the cataleptogenic effect of neuroleptics (Davies and Williams, 1978; Biggio et al., 1977; Keller et al., 1976; Worms and Lloyd,

Table 6 Effects of ECS on Met-enkephalin concentration in various brain regions

Region	Control	ECS × 10	Sub con × 10	ECS × 1	Sub con × 1
N. caudatus	9.5 ± 0.74	16.0 ± 0.90*	9.9 ± 0.85	9.5 ± 1.0	9.3 ± 1.2
Cortex	0.50 ± 0.050	0.62 ± 0.070	0.45 ± 0.060	0.52 ± 0.060	0.60 ± 0.040
Medulla and pons	2.5 ± 0.30	2.6 ± 0.40	2.2 ± 0.30	2.0 ± 0.20	2.6 ± 0.40

Met-enkephalin content as ng mg protein^{-1}
*$p < 0.05$ compared to controls, ECS conditions as for Table 5

1978). Conversely drugs which decrease GABA function, i.e. picrotoxin, bicuc-culine, and allylglycine, decrease haloperidol-induced catalepsy (Worms and Lloyd, 1978; Green *et al.*, 1979). Therefore it was decided to examine the effects of ECS on haloperidol-induced catalepsy. Full experimental details are published elsewhere (Green *et al.*, 1979); the scoring system is described in Table 1.

At 12 h after a single electroconvulsive shock, the catalepsy response was un-altered. However, the response was markedly attenuated 24 h after the shock. At 48 h after the ECS the response was normal again. Following ECS X 5 (over five days) there was inhibition of the cataleptic response at both 24 h and 48 h after the shock while the normal response was seen at 72 h (Figure 5). After ECS once daily for ten days there was an attenuated response 24 h and 72 h later with the response being near normal by seven days. Sub-convulsive shocks for ten days had no effect (Figure 6).

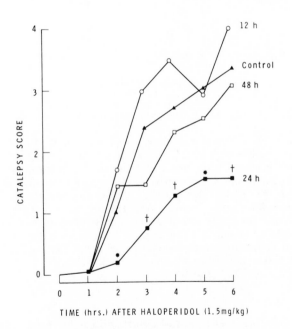

TIME (hrs.) AFTER HALOPERIDOL (1.5mg/kg)

Figure 5.   Cataleptic response to haloperidol at various times following a single ECS per day for five days. Rats were given ECS treatment and the cataleptic response during 6 h following haloperi-dol (1.5 mg kg^{-1}) measured 12 h (○), 24 h (■), and 48 h (□) after the shock. Anaesthetic only (control) response (▲). Significant differences from the con-trol response *$p < 0.01$, †$p < 0.001$. Number of animals: control, 9; 12 h, 6; 24 h, 17; 48 h, 8

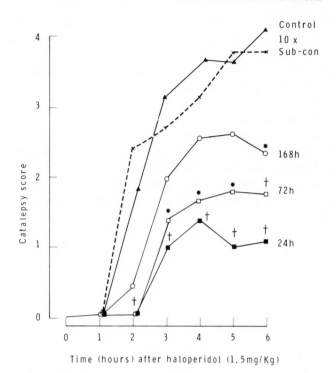

Figure 6.   Cataleptic response to haloperidol at various times following a single ECS a day for ten days. Rats were given ECS treatment and the cataleptic response during 6 h following haloperidol (1.5 mg kg^{-1}) measured 24 h (■), 72 h (□) and 168 h (○) after the final shock. Anaesthetic only (control) response (▲) and cataleptic response 24 h after the final shock of ten subconvulsive shocks (one daily for ten days) (X) also shown. Significant differences from the control response: *$p < 0.01$, †$p < 0.001$. Number of animals: control, 13; 24 h, 16; 72 h, 8; 168 h, 7; subcon, 6

It appears, therefore, that effects of a single ECS are consolidated and therefore last longer following further ECS treatments. This is consistent with the conditions thought necessary for a clinical response to ECT, i.e. both the number of treatments and the overall time involved are important for the improvement (Kety, 1974; Fink, 1974).

The length of time of the changed responses following ECS X 10 is similar to the length of time over which enhanced monoaminergic responses are seen.

It is attractive to ascribe the changed monoaminergic behavioural responses on

ECS to altered GABA function. However, changes in NAergic function and turnover also occur following ECS (Modigh, 1975, 1976) and may be involved in the altered responses as NA appears to influence neuroleptic-induced catalepsy (Honma and Fukashima, 1977; Al-Shabibi and Doggett, 1978; Zabrowska-Lapina, 1977). Also the sequential inter-relationships of the behavioural and biochemical effects of ECS are unknown—are the changed aminergic responses due to GABA and perhaps met-enkephalin changes or do the latter alter because of some initial change in the monoaminergic systems? Furthermore, the relevance of such changes to the antidepressant mechanism of ECT is going to be difficult to ascertain. It may however be possible to investigate whether ECT alters transmitter function in man by neuroendocrinological methods. Initial work (Eden and Modigh, 1977) suggests such an approach may be possible. Eventually such data may provide information that will lead to new pharmacological treatments for depression with the high efficacy of ECT but, perhaps, with less serious side-effects on (for example) memory.

SUMMARY

The possible mechanism of antidepressant action of electroconvulsive therapy was investigated by examining the effects of electroconvulsive shock (ECS) on brain neurotransmitter biochemistry and on various behavioural models.

It was found that when rats were given a single electroconvulsive shock daily for ten days the monoamine-mediated behavioural responses which follow administration of tranylcypromine/L-tryptophan or tranylcypromine/L-Dopa were enhanced 24 h after the final convulsion. This indicated increased 5-hydroxytryptamine and dopamine function respectively. The enhanced responses appear to result from postsynaptic changes since behavioural responses to the 5-HT agonists 5-methoxy N,N-dimethyltryptamine and quipazine and the dopamine agonist apomorphine were also enhanced. Enhanced responses are seen when the ECS is given in ways closely mimicking the clinical administration of ECT. Thus responses were enhanced in rats given ECS over ten days both anaesthetized and given a muscle relaxant, and when the electrodes were placed unilaterally or bilaterally. Responses were also enhanced after flurothyl convulsions as well as after ECS. Enhanced responses were not seen after sub-convulsive shocks, after repeated ECS during one day only, or using electrodes applied to the feet.

Repeated ECS decreased GABA turnover in the n.accumbens and n.caudatus and also produced regional changes in brain met-enkephalin concentrations. Further evidence for a functional change in brain GABA systems was that ECS decreases neuroleptic-induced catalepsy, as this also followed administration of GABA antagonists. The possibility that these changes result in the altered monoamine-mediated responses is discussed.

The possible contribution of these results to the development of a pharmacological treatment for depression with a similar efficacy to ECT is also discussed.

ACKNOWLEDGEMENTS

I gratefully acknowledge the stimulating collaboration of my colleagues in the experiments presented in this chapter. Most of the work was performed with Professor David G. Grahame-Smith and Drs David W. Costain, David J. Heal, and Christopher K. Atterwill in Oxford. The GABA turnover study and met[5]-enkephalin study was undertaken with Drs E. Costa, E. Peralta, C. C. Mao, and J. S. Hong in Washington D. C.

REFERENCES

Abrams, R. (1974) Multiple ECT: what have we learned? in Fink, M., Kety, S., McGaugh, J., and Williams, T. A. (eds.) *Psychobiology of Convulsive Therapy* V. H. Winston & Sons, Washington D.C., pp. 79–84.

Al-Shabibi, U. M. H., and Doggett, N. S. (1978) On the central noradrenergic mechanism involved in haloperidol-induced catalepsy. *J. Pharm. Pharmac.*, **30**, 529–531.

Avery, D., and Winokur, G. (1977) The efficacy of electroconvulsive therapy and antidepressants in depression. *Biological Psychiatry*, **12**, 507–523.

Bertilsson, L., and Costa, E. (1976) Mass fragmentographic quantitation of glutamic acid and γ-aminobutyric acid in cerebella nuclei and sympathetic ganglia of rats. *J. Chromat.*, **118**, 395–402.

Bertilsson, L., Mao, C. C., and Costa, E. (1977) Application of principles of steady state kinetics to the estimation of γ-aminobutyric acid turnover rate in nuclei of rat brain. *J. Pharmac. exp. Ther.*, **200**, 277–282.

Biggio, G., Casu, M., Corda, M. G., Vernaleone, F., and Gessa, G. L. (1977) Effect of Muscimol, a GABA-mimetic agent, on dopamine metabolism in the mouse brain. *Life Sci.*, **21**, 525–532.

Burt, D. R., Creese, E., and Snyder, S. H. (1977) Antischizophrenic drugs: chronic treatment elevates dopamine receptor binding in brain. *Science*, **196**, 326–328.

Costa, E. (1977) Some recent advances in the biochemical pharmacology of γ-aminobutyric acid, in Usdin, E., Hamburg, D. A., and Barchas, J. D. (eds.) *Neuroregulators and Psychiatric Disorders*. Oxford University Press, New York, pp. 372–390.

Costain, D. W., Green, A. R., and Grahame-Smith, D. G. (1979) Enhanced 5-hydroxytryptamine-mediated behavioural responses in rats following repeated electroconvulsive shock: relevance to the mechanism of the antidepressive effect of electroconvulsive therapy. *Psychopharmacology*, **61**, 167–170.

Cott, J., and Engel, J. (1977) Suppression by GABAergic drugs of the locomotor stimulation induced by morphine amphetamine and apomorphine: evidence for both pre- and post-synaptic inhibition of catecholamine systems. *J. Neural Transm.*, **40**, 253–268.

Davies, J. A., and Williams, J. (1978) The effect of baclofen on α-flupenthixol-induced catalepsy in the rat. *Br. J. Pharmc.*, **62**, 303–305.

Drug Ther. Bull. (1977) When should ECT be used? *Drug Ther. Bull.*, **15**, 2–4.

Eden, S., and Modigh, K. (1977) Effects of apomorphine and clonidine on rat plasma growth hormone after pretreatment with reserpine and electroconvulsive shocks. *Brain Res.*, **129**, 379–383.

Evans, J. P. M., Grahame-Smith, D. G., Green, A. R., and Tordoff, A. F. C. (1976) Electroconvulsive shock increases the behavioural responses of rats to brain

5-hydroxytryptamine accumulation and central nervous system stimulant drugs. *Br. J. Pharmac.*, **56**, 193–199.

Fink, M. (1974) Induced seizures and human behaviour, in Fink, M., Kety, S., McGaugh, J., and Williams, T. A. (eds.) *Psychobiology of Convulsive Therapy.* V. H. Winston & Sons, Washington, D.C., pp. 1–17.

Fink, M., Kahn, R. L., Karp, E., Pollack, M., Green, M. A., Allan, B., and Lefkowits, H. J. (1961) Inhalant-induced convulsions. Significance for the theory of the convulsive therapy process. *Arch. gen. Psychiat.*, **4**, 259–266.

Freund, D. J., and Warren, F. Z. (1965) The clinical impression of hexaflurodiethylether (Indoklon) following more than 800 treatments. (Preliminary report). *Dis. Nerv. System*, **25**, 56–57.

Grahame-Smith, D. G., Green, A. R., and Costain, D. W. (1978) Mechanism of the antidepressant action of electroconvulsive therapy. *Lancet*, i, 254–256.

Green, A. R. (1978a) Repeated exposure of rats to the convulsant agent flurothyl enhances 5-hydroxytryptamine- and dopamine-mediated behavioural responses. *Br. J. Pharmac.*, **62**, 325–331.

Green, A. R. (1978b) ECT–How does it work? *TINS*, **1**, 53–54.

Green, A. R., Bloomfield, M. R., Atterwill, C. K., and Costain, D. W. (1979) Electroconvulsive shock reduces the cataleptogenic effect of both haloperidol and arecoline in rats. *Neuropharmacology*, **18**, 447–451.

Green, A. R., and Costain, D. W. (1978) The biochemistry of depression, in Paykel, E., and Coppen, A. (eds.) *Psychopharmacology of Affective Disorders.* British Association of Psychopharmacology Monograph. Oxford University Press, Oxford, pp. 14–40.

Green, A. R., and Grahame-Smith, D. G. (1976) Effects of drugs on the processes regulating the functional activity of brain 5-hydroxytryptamine. *Nature*, **260**, 487–491.

Green, A. R., and Grahame-Smith, D. G. (1978) Processes regulating the functional activity of brain 5-hydroxytryptamine: results of animal experimentation and their relevance to the understanding and treatment of depression. *Pharmakopsychiat.*, **11**, 3–16.

Green, A. R., Heal, D. J., and Grahame-Smith, D. G. (1977) Further observations on the effect of repeated electroconvulsive shock on the behavioural responses of rats produced by increases in the functional activity of brain 5-hydroxytryptamine and dopamine. *Psychopharmacology*, **52**, 195–200.

Green, A. R., and Kelly, P. H. (1976) Evidence concerning the involvement of 5-hydroxytryptamine in the locomotor activity produced by amphetamine or tranylcypromine plus L-dopa *Br. J. Pharmac.*, **57**, 141–147.

Green, A. R., Peralta, E., Hong, J. S., Mao, C. C., Atterwill, C. K., and Costa, E. (1978) Alterations in GABA metabolism and Met-enkephalin contents in rat brain following repeated electroconvulsive shocks. *J. Neurochem.*, **31**, 607–611.

Green, A. R., Tordoff, A. F. C., and Bloomfield, M. R. (1976) Elevation of brain GABA concentrations with aminooxyacetic acid: effect on the hyperactivity syndrome produced by increased 5-hydroxytryptamine synthesis in rats. *J. Neural Transm.*, **39**, 103–112.

Haefely, W., Kulcsar, A., Mohler, H., Pieri, L., Polc, P., and Schaffner, R. (1975) Possible involvement of GABA in the central actions of benzodiazepines, in Costa, E., and Greengard, P. (eds.) *Mechanism of Action of Benzodiazepines*, Raven Press, New York, pp. 131–151.

Heal, D. J., and Green, A. R. (1978) Repeated electroconvulsive shock increases the behavioural responses of rats to injection of both dopamine and dibutyryl cyclic AMP into the nucleus accumbens. *Neuropharmacology*, **17**, 1085-1087.

Honma, T., and Fukashima, H. (1977) Role of brain norepinephrine in neuroleptic-induced catalepsy in rats. *Pharmac. Biochem. Behav.*, **7**, 501-506.

Karliner, W., and Padula, L. (1959a) Improved technique for Indoklon convulsive therapy. *Am. J. Psychiat.*, **116**, 358.

Karliner, W., and Padula, L. (1959b) Indoklon combined with pentothal and Anectine. *Am. J. Psychiat.*, **115**, 1041-1042.

Keller, H. H., Schaffner, R., and Haefely, W. (1976) Interactions of benzodiazepines with neuroleptics at central dopamine neurones. *Naunyn-Schmiedeberg's Arch. Pharmac.*, **294**, 1-7.

Kety, S. S. (1974) Biochemical and neurochemical effects of electroconvulsive shock, in Fink, M., Kety, S., McGaugh, J., and Williams, T. A. (eds.) *Psychobiology of Convulsive Therapy*. V. H. Winston & Sons, Washington, D.C., pp. 285-294.

Krantz, J. C., Esquibel, A., Truitt, E. B., Ling, A. S. C., and Kurland, A. A. (1958) Hexafluorodiethylether (Indoklon)—an inhalant convulsant—its use in psychiatric treatment. *J. Am. med. Assoc.* **166**, 1555-1562.

Lancaster, W. P., Steinhert, R. R., and Frost, I. (1958) Unilateral electroconvulsive therapy. *J. Ment. Sci.*, **104**, 221-227.

Mao, C. C., Marco, E., Revuelta, A., Bertilsson, L., and Costa, E. (1977) The turnover rate of γ-aminobutyric acid in the nuclei of telencephalon: implications in the pharmacology of antipsychotics and of a minor tranquilizer. *Biol. Psychiat.*, **12**, 359-371.

Modigh, K. (1975) Electroconvulsive shock and post-synaptic catecholamine effects: increased psychomotor stimulant action of apomorphine and clonidine in reserpine pretreated mice by repeated ECS. *J. Neural. Transm.*, **36**, 19-32.

Modigh, K. (1976) Long-term effects of electroconvulsive shock therapy on synthesis turnover and uptake of brain monoamines. *Psychopharmacology*, **49**, 179-185.

Naik, S. R., Guidotti, A., and Costa, E. (1976) Central GABA receptor agonists: comparison of Muscimol and baclofen. *Neuropharmacology*, **15**, 479-484.

Ottosson, J.-O. (1960) Experimental studies of the mode of action of electroconvulsive therapy. *Acta psychiat. Neurol. Scand.*, **Suppl. 145**, 1-141.

Pollard. H., Llorens-Cortes, C., and Schwartz, J. L. (1977) Enkephalin receptors on dopaminergic neurones in rat striatum. *Nature*, **268**, 745-747.

Royal College of Psychiatrists. (1977) The Royal College of Psychiatrists memorandum on the use of electroconvulsive therapy. *Br. J. Psychiat.*, **131**, 261-272.

Seager, C. J. (1959) Controlled trial of straight and modified electroplexy. *J. Ment. Sci.*, **105**, 1022-1028.

Spreche, D. A. (1964) A quantitative comparison of electroconvulsive therapy with hexafluorodiethylether. *J. Neuropsychiat.*, **5**, 132-137.

Turek, I. S., and Hanlon, T. E. (1977) The effectiveness and safety of electroconvulsive therapy (ECT). *J. Nerv. Ment. Dis.*, **164**, 419-431.

Ungerstedt, U. (1971) Postsynaptic supersensitivity after 6-hydroxydopamine induced degeneration of the nigrostriatal dopamine system in the rat brain. *Acta Physiol. Scand.*, **83 Suppl. 367**, 49-68.

Valentine, M., Keddie, K. M. G., and Dunne, D. (1968) A comparison of techniques in electroconvulsive therapy. *Br. J. Psychiat.*, **114**, 989-996.

Worms, P., and Lloyd, K. G. (1978) Influence of GABA-agonists and antagonists on neuroleptic-induced catalepsy in rats. *Life Sci.*, **23**, 475-478.

Zebrowska-Lupina, I. (1977) The effect of α-adrenolytics on central action of agonists and antagonists of dopaminergic system. *Pol. J. Pharmac. Pharm.*, **29**, 393-404.

The Biochemistry of Psychiatric Disturbances
Edited by G. Curzon
© 1980 John Wiley & Sons Ltd.

CHAPTER 4

Biochemical Abnormalities in Schizophrenia: the Dopamine Hypothesis

ERNEST G. S. SPOKES

INTRODUCTION

Although pathologists have deliberated over schizophrenic brains for many years, no consistent neuropathological abnormality has been defined in schizophrenia and it seems likely that the underlying lesion has a biochemical basis. This is not a novel concept, for nearly 100 years ago Thudichum proposed that madness might arise from a chemical imbalance in the brain (Thudichum, 1884). Numerous hypotheses have been proposed concerning the nature of this biochemical abnormality. With the elucidation of the chemical structures of hallucinogenic drugs some 20 to 30 years ago, Osmond and Smythies (1952) noted these agents bore a close chemical similarity to putative neurotransmitters, but possessed additional methyl groups. For example, mescaline and amphetamine are phenylalkylamine derivatives with a similar structure to the catecholamines (DA, NA, and adrenaline), whereas D-lysergic acid diethylamide and psilocybin are tryptamine derivatives resembling 5-HT. This led to various claims that schizophrenic subjects might, via an aberrant methylation pathway, produce an endogenous psychotomimetic substance detectable in urine. In 1962, Friedhoff and van Winkle reported the presence of 3, 4-dimethoxyphenylethylamine, a non-hallucinogenic DA derivative but structurally closely related to mescaline, in the urine of schizophrenic patients and suggested it might be a metabolite of a psychotomimetic precursor. However, it was later shown that the excretion of this compound is under both drug and dietary influences to which institutionalized schizophrenics are often exposed. Moreover it can be found in the urine of normal individuals. On the whole, the direct search for a 'toxic metabolite' in schizophrenia has proved unrewarding (reviews: Kety, 1967; Matthysse and Lipinski, 1975; Smythies, 1976).

Another approach adopted by workers investigating the possibility that an abnormally methylated amine might be implicated in schizophrenia has been to administer methionine, a methyl group donor, to schizophrenic patients. Several groups of workers have reported that this exacerbated schizophrenic symptoms (Pollin et al., 1961; Alexander et al., 1963; Kety, 1967; Antun et al., 1971). However, no adequate studies have yet been performed on normal control subjects; nor is it clear whether the psychosis represents an exacerbation of the schizophrenic illness or a superimposed toxic psychosis.

In the past ten years or so a more fruitful approach to schizophrenia research has emerged, based on the clues obtained from neuropharmacological studies, and implicating the neurotransmitter DA as having a critical role in the schizophrenic illness. In particular, drugs which are effective in reversing some symptoms of schizophrenia possess a common property of antagonizing the effects of DA at central synapses. On the other hand, drugs which potentiate or mimic DA transmission may exacerbate symptoms. These observations have led to the 'DA hypothesis', which proposes that schizophrenia may be associated with a functional overactivity of DAergic pathways in the brain.

DAERGIC SYSTEMS IN THE BRAIN

In 1962, Falck, Hillarp and coworkers developed a histofluorometric technique for visualizing neurons containing monoamines (DA, NA, and 5-HT) in the brain. This technique incorporates the condensation of these monoamines in tissue sections with formaldehyde to form intensely fluorescent isoquinolines. In this way, cell bodies, axons, and nerve terminals of the monoamine-containing neurons have been mapped throughout the central nervous system, a discovery which heralded a new era in functional neuroanatomy. The present chapter is concerned with DAergic systems, and only these will be described.

The distribution of DA-containing neurons in mammalian brain is well documented, and three main DAergic tracts have been identified: the nigro-striatal pathway, arising from pigmented cell bodies in the pars compacta of the substantia nigra and projecting rostrally to the subdivisions of the corpus striatum (caudate nucleus, putamen, and globus pallidus) (Andén et al., 1964; Poirier and Sourkes, 1965; Ungerstedt, 1971); the so-called 'mesolimbic' and 'mesocortical' pathways, arising from cell bodies dorsal to the interpeduncular nucleus of the midbrain and ascending to the nuclear and cortical components of the limbic system, such as the nucleus accumbens, olfactory tubercle (anterior perforated substance), septal nuclei, amygdala, and cingulate gyrus (Ungerstedt, 1971; Lindvall and Björklund, 1974); and the tuberoinfundibular system, consisting of short-axoned neurons with cell bodies in the arcuate and periventricular nuclei of the hypothalamus and fibres descending to the median eminence (Björklund et al., 1970). An outline of these presumed pathways in human brain is shown semi-diagrammatically in Figure 1. Of these DA-containing systems, the nigrostriatal pathway has been most extensively studied and contains about 75% of the total brain DA in most mammals.

Biosynthesis and metabolism of DA in the brain

The synthesis of DA proceeds as follows: tyrosine → Dopa → DA. Tyrosine taken up into catecholamine neurons is hydroxylated to dihydroxyphenylalanine (Dopa)

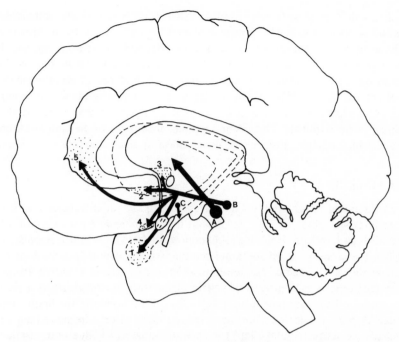

Figure 1. A semi-diagrammatic representation of presumed DAergic pathways in human brain. A: nigrostriatal pathway; B: mesolimbic pathway; C: tuberoinfundibular system. Stippled areas denote limbic regions: (1) amygdala; (2) nucleus accumbens; (3) septal nuclei; (4) anterior perforated substance; (5) anterior cingulate gyrus

by tyrosine hydroxylase (TOH) which requires a biopterin cofactor (Nagatsu *et al.*, 1964). In the brain this enzyme occurs exclusively in catecholamine neurons and its activity is rate-limiting for catecholamine synthesis (Levitt *et al.*, 1965) and is controlled by end-product inhibition (Weiner, 1970). Thus, under conditions of increased nerve firing, the catecholamines are released and TOH acts more efficiently in synthesizing Dopa. Conversely, when the nerve is resting and intraneuronal concentrations of catecholamines are high, TOH activity is reduced. These adaptive changes in TOH activity are effected by alterations in the kinetic properties of the enzyme with respect to its affinity for the substrate tyrosine and pteridine cofactor. Dopa is decarboxylated to DA by Dopa decarboxylase (aromatic amino acid decarboxylase) a widely distributed enzyme. These foregoing reactions occur in the neuronal cytosol after which DA is concentrated in storage vesicles. In NAergic neurons, the storage vesicles contain a further enzyme, dopamine-β-hydroxylase, which converts DA to NA (Kaufman and Friedman, 1965).

DA is metabolized via two pathways: deamination by monoamine oxidase; and O-methylation by catechol-O-methyltransferase which transfers a methyl group from S-adenosylmethionine to the *meta*-hydroxyl of catecholamines. Both enzymes occur in a wide variety of tissues as well as in nerve cells and have been extensively studied by Axelrod (1965). Monoamine oxidase is bound to the outer membrane of mitochondria, and in the central nervous system is found in neurons and glia. In monoamine-containing nerve endings it is believed to deaminate surplus monoamine that leaks out of synaptic vesicles, and under physiological conditions probably has little effect on the amount of DA, or other monoamines, available for release. Catechol-O-methyltransferase seems to be located largely outside catecholamine-containing nerve terminals. The major cerebral metabolites of DA are HVA and dopacetic acid, the latter substance usually in relatively small amounts.

Release and uptake of DA

Most of the initial information on the release and uptake of catecholamines from nerve endings was obtained from studies on the sympathetic nervous system and adrenal medulla (Axelrod, 1965; Weinshilboum et al., 1971). These studies indicated that when the nerves or gland are stimulated the resulting depolarization of the cell membrane allows entrance of calcium ions which trigger release of catecholamines from storage vesicles by a process of reverse pinocytosis or exocytosis. It is likely that a similar calcium-dependent mechanism for release occurs in the brain. After the catecholamine is released from the nerve ending its effects are rapidly terminated mainly by active re-uptake into the nerve terminal by a high affinity, sodium-dependent mechanism (Iversen, 1970).

Postsynaptic DA receptors

DA released from presynaptic terminals diffuses across the synaptic cleft and binds to specific postsynaptic receptors. DA receptors are pharmacologically distinct from α- or β-adrenergic receptors for NA and adrenaline. They are potently stimulated by apomorphine and bromocriptine, but are unaffected by α- or β-adrenergic agonists or antagonists. Interaction of DA with its receptor leads to activation of DA-sensitive adenyl cyclase and cAMP is formed (Iversen, 1975). However, recent studies have shown that not all DA receptors have this property. For example, autoreceptors for DA on cell bodies and terminals of nigrostriatal neurons and DA receptors on prolactin-secreting cells do not stimulate adenyl cyclase (review: Kebabian and Calne, 1979). Thus at least two classes of DA receptor exist in brain.

PHARMACOLOGY OF DAERGIC SYSTEMS

(i) Amphetamines

Connell (1958) was the first to describe the close similarity between amphetamine-induced psychosis (in 42 cases) and acute or chronic paranoid schizophrenia. Although amphetamine psychosis resembles schizophrenia in many respects, it differs from schizophrenia in that olfactory and visual hallucinations, emotional excitement and absence of a formal thought disorder are more common. However, it is now generally accepted that amphetamine psychosis provides the most accurate drug-induced 'model schizophrenia' (Snyder, 1973). Moreover, d-amphetamine can exacerbate a schizophrenic illness (Janowsky et al., 1977).

Pharmacological studies indicate that amphetamine enhances DAergic neurotransmission by displacing DA from storage vesicles and blocking re-uptake into the presynaptic terminals (Azzaro and Rutledge, 1973). That amphetamine administration results in excess DA release in man, is supported by the study of Angrist et al. (1974) who showed that it led to a rise in HVA concentration in lumbar CSF.

In experimental animals amphetamine causes locomotor hyperactivity and stereotyped behaviour (Randrup and Munkvad, 1967). These can be prevented by (a) pretreatment with α-methyl-para-tyrosine (a competitive inhibitor of TOH) which reduces levels of DA (Randrup and Munkvad, 1966) (b) destruction of central DAergic pathways by microinjection of 6-hydroxydopamine, a selective neurotoxin for DAergic neurons (Creese and Iversen, 1975), and (c) treatment with neuroleptic drugs which block postsynaptic DA receptors (Randrup and Munkvad, 1965). It is apparent, therefore, that much of the behavioural change induced by amphetamine in animals is dependent on increased amounts of DA at central synapses.

(ii) Antipsychotic drugs

The introduction of antipsychotic drugs (neuroleptics) for the treatment of schizophrenia has had a profound impact in psychiatry and neuropharmacology. The observation that these compounds exerted specific antipsychotic effects suggested that schizophrenia had a biochemical basis which was amenable to modification. In recent years, compelling pharmacological evidence has accumulated that the one property shared by neuroleptics of the three major chemical classes, phenothiazines, butyrophenones, and thioxanthenes, is the ability to act as competitive antagonists at DA receptors.

Suggestive correlations exist between the ability of neuroleptics to block the behavioural effects of amphetamine or DA agonists in animals and the relative potencies of the same drugs in treating schizophrenia (Janssen et al., 1967). The discovery of DA-sensitive adenyl cyclase in brain made it possible to examine drugs as agonists and antagonists for DA receptors in vitro (Figure 2). Using this test system, it was found that antipsychotic drugs potently antagonized the stimulation of cAMP formation by DA (Iversen, 1975). However, although a good correlation is found between the ability of phenothiazines and thioxanthenes to inhibit DA-stimulated adenyl cyclase and their in vivo potencies, the butyrophenones are relatively weak antagonists in this system, but have high clinical potency. Recently, Seeman et al., (1976) and Creese et al. (1976) found that [³H]haloperidol, a butyrophenone, binds to postsynaptic DA receptors in striatal tissue and that the ability of neuroleptic drugs, of all chemical classes, to inhibit this in vitro correlates strongly

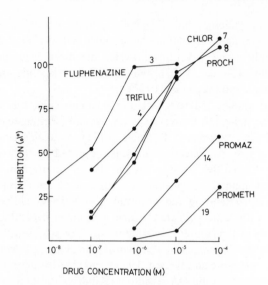

DRUG CONCENTRATION (M)

Figure 2. Effect of phenothiazines on DA-stimulated cAMP production in striatal homogenates. Basal level of cAMP production was 45.5 ± 3.6 pmol per sample (2 mg wet weight) and stimulated (100 μM DA) was 88.7 ± 9.1 pmol per sample (means $\pm$ S.E.M. for six experiments). Each point is the mean of at least five separate incubations. At 10^{-4} M some drugs inhibited basal cAMP production; this is represented as an inhibition of more than 100%. Abbreviations: TRIFLU, trifluoperazine; CHLOR, chlorpromazine; PROCH, prochlorperazine; PROMAZ, promazine; PROMETH; promethazine. Reproduced with permission from Iversen, 1975. Copyright 1975 by the American Association for the Advancement of Science

with clinical potency (Figure 3). It has been proposed that these binding procedures should provide a simple and specific means to evaluate neuroleptic drugs.

Burt *et al.* (1976) have suggested that the differences in the relative effects of neuroleptics on DA-sensitive adenyl cyclase and [^{3}H]haloperidol binding result from DA receptors having different 'agonist' and 'antagonist' conformations. However, Leysen and Laduron (1977) found that haloperidol binding sites and DA-sensitive adenyl cyclase have different subcellular distributions which suggests that they are physically separate, and consistent with the view that more than one type of DA receptor exists in brain.

Various *in vivo* effects on DAergic systems provide further evidence that neuro-

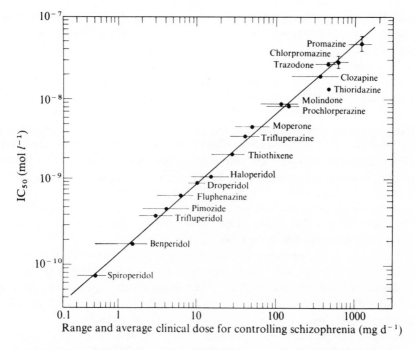

Figure 3. Comparison of the clinical potencies of neuroleptic drugs, measured as average daily dose in treating schizophrenia, with potencies of the same drugs in displacing [³H]haloperidol from DA receptor binding sites *in vitro* (concentration of drug required to displace 50% of specific haloperidol binding). Reproduced from Seeman *et al.*, 1976 by permission of *Nature*

leptics act as DA antagonists. One example is provided by their actions on the nigrostriatal DAergic and striatal cholinergic systems. It is now generally accepted that at least some DAergic terminals in the striatum synapse with cholinergic interneurons (Hattori *et al.*, 1976) which they inhibit (Bloom *et al.*, 1965; Connor, 1970; Feltz and DeChamplain, 1972; McLennan and York, 1967) by a tonic release of DA (Guyenet *et al.*, 1975). In Parkinson's disease the pigmented cells of the substantia nigra degenerate (Hassler, 1938) so that DA is lost from the striatum (Ehringer and Hornykiewicz, 1960) and cholinergic cells, released from inhibition, become more active. At least some features of parkinsonism result from excessive stimulation of neurons which are responsive to acetylcholine.

Neuroleptic drugs are well known to produce iatrogenic parkinsonism and in experimental animals cause increased acetylcholine release in the striatum (Bartholini *et al.*, 1975; Pletscher, 1976), increased DA turnover and increased firing of nigral DAergic cells (Bunney and Aghajanian, 1975). These effects can be antagonized not only by DA agonists (Ladinsky *et al.*, 1974) but also by anticholinergic drugs (Pletscher, 1976) as cholinergic neurons in the striatum appear to exert a positive feedback effect on DAergic cells (Pletscher, 1976), possibly acting both presynaptically (Westfall, 1974a, b) and via GABA-containing striato-nigral and pallido-nigral pathways (Bunney and Aghajanian, 1976).

Thus both iatrogenic parkinsonism and its amelioration by anticholinergic compounds can be explained on the basis of postsynaptic DA receptor blockade. In general the relative clinical potencies of neuroleptic drugs correlate well with their ability to induce parkinsonism. However, thioridazine (Cole and Clyde, 1961) and clozapine (Bürki et al., 1975) have disproportionately weak parkinsonian-inducing effects relative to their antipsychotic potency, and only weakly increase DA turnover in the striatum (Stawarz et al., 1975), observations that they have been taken as evidence against the 'DA hypothesis' of schizophrenia. However, both these drugs have intrinsic anticholinergic properties and are potent antimuscarinic agents (Miller and Hiley, 1974; Snyder et al., 1974), which explains the low incidence of parkinsonism associated with their use.

Another in vivo consequence of DA antagonism by neuroleptics is their effect on plasma prolactin levels. DA in the tuberoinfundibular system inhibits the release of prolactin from the anterior pituitary. Thus drugs which enhance DAergic effects such as L-Dopa, apomorphine or bromocriptine inhibit prolactin release whereas neuroleptics increase circulating prolactin levels (Frantz and Sachar, 1976). Recently, it has been reported that prolactin responses to neuroleptic drugs correlate well with their antischizophrenic potencies (Langer et al., 1977) and it has been suggested that plasma prolactin levels may be a useful indicator of DA receptor blockade.

These findings strongly support the argument that DA blockade is involved in the antischizophrenic actions of neuroleptic drugs. A number of other properties of these drugs do not now seem very relevant. Some 15 years ago, electron donor activity, inhibition of oxidative phosphorylation, and membrane 'stabilization' were considered to be the most likely mediators of the antischizophrenic action of phenothiazines (Guth and Spirtes, 1964). Since these drugs have a high lipid solubility, they concentrate in membranes and, in high concentration, disrupt metabolic processes in membrane systems. However, these actions are shared equally by anti-psychotic and non-antipsychotic phenothiazines (Foster and Fyfe, 1966). Moreover, the non-antipsychotic phenothiazines are ineffective in blocking DA-sensitive adenyl cyclase or haloperidol binding in the test systems already discussed. Neither do they markedly increase striatal DA turnover (Matthysse, 1974).

Some phenothiazines, including chlorpromazine, have antihistamine and α-adrenergic receptor blocking actions. The antimuscarinic effect of certain neuroleptics has already been mentioned, and some may bind to 5-HT receptors (Enna et al., 1976); however, as these properties are not shared by all neuroleptics, they are unlikely to be primarily responsible for antipsychotic actions, although the possibility that they may contribute to these actions is not excluded.

Although the anatomical site or sites of the central biochemical disturbance in schizophrenia are unknown, circumstantial evidence suggests that the limbic system may be involved (Stevens, 1973) and that neuroleptics exert their antipsychotic actions by blocking the DA receptors on the target neurons of the mesolimbic DAergic pathway, rather than in the striatum (Crow et al., 1977).

POST-MORTEM STUDIES ON HUMAN BRAIN TISSUE

One way of testing the 'DA hypothesis' of schizophrenia lies in biochemical studies on post-mortem brain tissue obtained from schizophrenic patients. In previous biochemical studies on human post-mortem brain abnormalities in neurotransmitters or related enzymes have been detected in a variety of neurological diseases, including Parkinson's disease (Ehringer and Hornykiewicz, 1960), Huntington's chorea (Bird and Iversen, 1974), and senile dementia (Perry et al., 1977; Bowen et al., 1976; Davies and Maloney, 1976).

In our laboratory we have undertaken biochemical studies on post-mortem material from 50 patients who died with a hospital diagnosis of schizophrenia. Our previous experience with human post-mortem biochemical research suggested that analyses of large numbers of pathological and control samples were necessary before firm conclusions could be reached, because of the considerable individual variations and the many uncontrollable ante- and post-mortem factors which influence such results (Spokes, 1979).

Various biochemical measurements are useful in human post-mortem neurochemical studies: (a) the concentrations of neurotransmitters and their metabolites —the latter values give some insight into transmitter turnover; (b) the activities of biosynthetic enzymes—these provide markers for specific cell populations; (c) activities of enzymes which degrade neurotransmitters; and (d) the affinity and density of postsynaptic receptors using specific binding of radioactively-labelled receptor ligands.

In our own studies, so far we have measured DA, NA, glutamic acid decarboxylase (GAD) (as a marker for GABA-containing neurons), and choline acetyltransferase (CAT) (as a marker for cholinergic neurons) in a variety of brain regions. These substances were chosen because the known interactions between DA, GABA, and acetylcholine in the basal ganglia suggested that similar relationships might be important in the limbic system.

No significant differences were found in any brain region for NA, CAT, or GAD (after allowing for ante-mortem factors). Significantly high DA concentrations were observed, however, in two limbic regions, the nucleus accumbens (+34%) and the anterior perforated substance (+95%), but not in other limbic areas (septal nuclei and amygdala) or in the striatum (Table 1) (Bird et al., 1979). In contrast, Crow and his colleagues (Crow et al., 1978, 1979; Owen et al., 1978) failed to detect significantly high DA concentrations in the nucleus accumbens from 16 patients who had died with schizophrenic illness, but reported significantly high DA and NA concentrations in the caudate nucleus. Like us, they failed to observe significant abnormalities in the putamen. The reasons for these discrepancies are not clear

Table 1. DA concentrations in post-mortem brain from patients with a hospital diagnosis of schizophrenia

| | Control | Schizophrenia |
	μg g protein^{-1}	
Putamen	22.0 ± 2.30(29)	22.9 ± 2.20(37)
Caudate	17.3 ± 1.27(51)	19.7 ± 1.35(50)
Nucleus accumbens	12.2 ± 0.95(46)	16.3 ± 1.03(51)†
Anterior perforated substance	1.9 ± 0.30(32)	3.7 ± 0.58(37)*
Septal nuclei	1.4 ± 0.14(35)	1.6 ± 0.15(32)
Amygdala central nucleus	5.4 ± 1.70(17)	3.9 ± 1.14(27)

Values are means and (S.E.M.) for the number of samples in brackets
*p <0.02 by Students t-test; p = 0.03 by Mann Whitney U-test
†p <0.005 by Students t-test; p = 0.0016 by Mann Whitney U-test

but may reflect differences in dissection procedures for the nucleus accumbens (Bird et al., 1979). We also found high NA concentrations in the nucleus accumbens of schizophrenics although the values were not significantly elevated. Farley and her colleagues have noted three-fold increases in NA concentration in the nucleus accumbens and ventral septum in post-mortem brain tissue from four schizophrenic subjects (Farley et al., 1978). The above evidence that NA levels are unchanged or even increased in schizophrenic brain tissue does not support the hypothesis of Wise and Stein (1973) that NA 'reward' pathways are damaged in schizophrenia. This was based on their finding of reduced dopamine-β-hydroxylase activity in post-mortem specimens of diencephalon from 18 schizophrenic patients, an observation not confirmed in subsequent studies (Wyatt et al., 1975; Cross et al., 1978).

Our findings of increased DA concentrations specifically in the nucleus accumbens and anterior perforated substance of post-mortem brain from schizophrenic patients are consistent with the hypothesis that an abnormality in mesolimbic DA pathways is involved in schizophrenia (Stevens, 1973). However, the present results must be interpreted with caution since an increased concentration of DA does not necessarily imply an increased density or activity of DAergic nerve terminals. Indeed, in animal experiments, raised DA levels can be associated with a reduction in activity of DAergic neurons (Walters and Roth, 1974). Moreover, such increases may be a consequence of long-term treatment with neuroleptic drugs. Indeed, studies in the rat have shown that chronic neuroleptic administration produces a selective increase in DA and NA concentration in the nucleus accumbens and septum (Lloyd et al., 1977), whereas levels in the striatum are unaffected (Lloyd et al., 1977; O'Keffe et al., 1970). However, in Huntington's chorea, a condition in which schizophrenic features may be prominent, recent work reveals highly significant DA increases in the corpus striatum and nucleus accumbens which do not appear to be explained by long-term neuroleptic drug administration (Spokes, 1980). It has been suggested that schizophrenia and Huntington's chorea have an anatomical–biochemical relationship (Klawans *et al.*, 1972) and it is possible that DAergic overactivity in the nucleus accumbens leads to the expression of psychotic features in both illnesses.

EVIDENCE AGAINST DAERGIC OVERACTIVITY IN SCHIZOPHRENIA

Despire the findings cited above there is still no convincing direct evidence for central DAergic hyperactivity in schizophrenia. Crow and his colleagues (1979) and Owen *et al.* (1978) did not find significantly raised values of DA metabolites in the brain of patients who had died with a schizophrenic illness. Indeed, HVA concentrations in the caudate nucleus were significantly low. Several groups of workers have been unable to detect significant abnormalities of HVA concentration in lumbar CSF of acute or chronic schizophrenic patients (Persson and Roos, 1969; Rimon *et al.*, 1971; Bowers, 1973; Post *et al.*, 1975). However, these values would probably be dominated by HVA secreted from nigrostriatal rather than limbic DAergic systems. There is some evidence that increasing symptoms in chronic schizophrenia are associated with decreasing prolactin secretion, suggesting the possibility of increased DA release from the tuberoinfundibular system (Johnstone *et al.*, 1977) but actual prolactin levels are reported to be normal in schizophrenia (Meltzer *et al.*, 1974).

Another possibility is that overactivity of central DAergic systems in schizophrenia could occur not through increased presynaptic activity but through a deficiency in an antagonistic system or through supersensitivity of postsynaptic DA receptors. There are a number of known analogies to the first possibility, i.e. that apparent DA overactivity arises from a defect in a neurotransmitter system which either normally inhibits DAergic neurons or which shares the same target neurons as the DA fibre but has antagonistic effects to DA. For example, some features of parkinsonism appear to result from striatal cholinergic overactivity but this is a consequence of loss of inhibitory DAergic fibres which innervate cholinergic neurons. Somewhat similarly, the apparent DAergic overactivity in the striatum in Huntington's chorea (Chase, 1973; Klawans and Weiner, 1974) may be a consequence of death of neurons, particularly those synthesising GABA, normally regulating DA release from nigrostriatal terminals which remain largely intact in this disease (Spokes, 1980). GABA deficiency has been postulated in schizophrenia (Roberts, 1972), and reduced GABA concentration in the schizophrenic nucleus accumbens has recently been reported (Perry *et al.*, 1979). We have reproduced this finding and have also demonstrated GABA depletion in the schizophrenic amygdala, values in other brain regions being normal (Spokes *et al.*, 1980). GABA is stable in post-mortem brain and, unlike GAD, is unaffected by agonal factors (Spokes *et al.*, 1979). Thus, it may be that measurements of GABA levels provide a more reliable index of the integrity of GABA systems than estimations of GAD.

The recent finding that the morphine-like peptide, β-endorphin, can, like neuroleptic drugs, cause catalepsy when injected into the rat brain has led to the suggestion that endogenous brain peptides of this class might be naturally occurring protective agents against psychosis, and that schizophrenia might be associated with a deficiency of such peptides (Jacquet and Marks, 1976). However, in a limited study on schizophrenic brain, levels of β-endorphin were similar to those in controls (Lightman et al., 1979).

Another possibility is an imbalance between DA and 5-HT systems in schizophrenia (Green and Grahame-Smith, 1976a; Smythies, 1976). It is interesting that propranolol, which may have beneficial effects in the treatment of chronic schizophrenia (Yorkston et al., 1974), appears to act as a central 5-HT antagonist without DA blocking actions (Green and Grahame-Smith, 1976b). However, measurements of 5-HT and its metabolites in post-mortem schizophrenic brain tissue have yielded values largely within the normal range (Crow et al., 1979; see, however, Chapter 8).

Evidence for postsynaptic DA receptor supersensitivity in schizophrenia has been equivocal. In vivo studies of growth hormone responses to apomorphine have revealed both supersensitive (Rotrosen et al., 1976) and normal responses (Ettigi et al., 1976). In studies on human post-mortem brain tissue, Carenzi et al. (1975) reported normal DA-sensitive adenyl cyclase activity, both basal and stimulated, in seven schizophrenic cases compared with eight normal controls. However, Lee et al. (1978) have recently reported highly significant increases in specific binding of [^{3}H]haloperidol in the striatum and nucleus accumbens of 20 schizophrenic patients which may indicate an increased density and/or increased affinity of receptors for haloperidol. This finding is consistent with Owen et al. (1978) who have found evidence of a substantial increase in DA receptor density in the striatum and nucleus accumbens, on the basis of specific spiroperidol binding, in brain tissue from schizophrenics. Attempts are now being made in our own and other laboratories to check these observations. However, even if confirmed, such abnormalities could result from neuroleptic treatment (Burt et al., 1977).

SUMMARY AND CONCLUSION

In recent years the most significant advance in the understanding of the biochemical basis of schizophrenia has come from the elucidation of the mode of action of drugs which ameliorate or exacerbate schizophrenic symptoms. This has given rise to the hypothesis that certain DAergic systems are functionally overactive in this disease. It now seems highly probable that the antipsychotic effect of neuroleptic drugs is mediated by blockade of postsynaptic DA receptors. Conversely the psychotomimetic properties of d-amphetamine appear to involve DA release and the blockade of DA re-uptake. It is not yet clear whether the above hypothesis is substantiated by our finding of increased DA concentrations in the nucleus accumbens and anterior perforated substance of post-mortem brain tissue from schizophrenic subjects.

The major gap in the 'DA hypothesis' is the lack of evidence for an absolute increase in DAergic activity, as reflected by elevated concentrations of DA metabolites. However, relative overactivity might occur through deficiences in antagonistic neurotransmitter systems or through DA receptor supersensitivity. It is reasonable to speculate that many schizophrenic symptoms are common expressions of different biochemical abnormalities in which relative DAergic overactivity is a common feature. If such biochemical heterogeneity does underlie the disease the action of neuroleptic drugs may turn out to be no more specific than that of a blood transfusion to an anaemic patient whose lack of red blood cells can be due to a myriad of causes but with essentially similar symptomatologies. It is possible, therefore, that with the accumulation of biochemical data, and with the use of multivariate analysis of results, biochemical subgroups will emerge. Consistent with this notion we have recently found that the activity of angiotensin-converting enzyme in the pars reticulata of the substantia nigra was significantly reduced in schizophrenia but only when the onset of the illness occurred between the ages of 15 and 24 years (Arregui et al., 1979). In the brain this enzyme is found intraneuronally, although little is understood of its functional significance (Arregui et al., 1978). This observation has led us to re-examine our raised DA and NA and reduced GABA values in the nucleus accumbens as a function of age of onset of schizophrenic illness. Preliminary results suggest that these abnormalities also are restricted to subjects whose illnesses began between the ages of 15 and 24 years.

Clearly these are fascinating times for investigators studying the biochemical abnormalities in schizophrenia. It is to be hoped that future studies in animals and on human post-mortem brain tissue will increase our understanding of neurotransmitter interactions in the CNS and elucidate further the biochemical mechanisms underlying the disease.

REFERENCES

Alexander, F., Curtis, G. C., Sprince, H., and Crosley, A. P. (1963) L-Methionine and L-tryptophane feedings in non-psychotic and schizophrenic patients with and without trancylpromine. *J. Nerv. Ment. Dis.*, **137**, 135–142.

Andén, N.-E., Carlsson, A., Dahlström, A., Fuxe, K., Hillarp, N. Å., and Larsson, N. (1964) Demonstration and mapping out of nigro-neostriatal dopamine neurones. *Life Sci.*, **3**, 523–530.

Angrist, B., Sathanathan, G., Wilk, S., and Gershon, S. (1974) Amphetamine psychosis; behavioural and biochemical aspects. *J. Psychiat. Res.*, **11**, 13–23.

Antun, F. T., Burnett, G. B., Cooper, A. J., Daly, R. J., Smythies, R. J., and Zeally, A. K. (1971) The effects of L-methionine (without MAOI) in schizophrenia. *J. Psychiat. Res.*, **8**, 63–71.

Arregui, A., Emson, P. C., and Spokes, E. G. (1978) Angiotensin-converting enzyme of substantia nigra: reduction of activity in Huntington's disease and after intrastriatal kainic acid in rat. *Eur. J. Pharmacol.*, **52**, 121–124.

Arregui, A., Mackay, A. V. P., Iversen, L. L., and Spokes, E. G. (1979) Reduction of angiotensin-converting enzyme in substantia nigra in early-onset schizophrenia. *N. Eng. J. Med.*, **300**, 502–503.

Axelrod, J. (1965) The metabolism, storage, and release of catecholamines. *Recent Prog. Horm. Res.*, **21**, 597–622.

Azzaro, A. J., and Rutledge, C. O. (1973) Selectivity of release of norepinephrine, dopamine and 5-hydroxytryptamine by amphetamine in various regions of rat brain. *Biochem. Pharmacol.*, **22**, 2801–2813.

Bartholini, G., Stadler, H., and Lloyd, K. G. (1975) Cholinergic-dopaminergic interregulations within the extrapyramidal system, in Waser P. G. (ed.), *Cholinergic Mechanisms*, Raven Press, New York, pp. 411–418.

Bird, E. D., and Iversen, L. L. (1974) Huntington's chorea: post-mortem measurement of glutamic acid decarboxylase, choline acetyltransferase and dopamine in basal ganglia. *Brain*, **97**, 457–472.

Bird, E. D., Spokes, E. G., and Iversen, L. L. (1979) Increased dopamine concentration in limbic areas of brain from patients dying with schizophrenia. *Brain*, **102**, 347–360.

Björklund, A., Falck, B., Hromek, F., Owman, C., and West, K. A. (1970) Identification and terminal distribution of the tubero-hypophyseal monoamine fibre systems in the rat by means of stereotaxic and microspectrofluorometric techniques. *Brain Res.*, **17**, 1–23.

Bloom, F. E., Costa, E., and Salmoiraghi, G. C. (1965) Anesthesia and the responsiveness of individual neurons of the caudate nucleus of the cat to acetylcholine, norepinephrine, and dopamine administered by microelectrophoresis. *J. Pharmacol. exp. Ther.*, **50**, 244–252.

Bowen, D. M., Smith, C. B., White, P., and Davison, A. N. (1976) Neurotransmitter-related enzymes and indices of hypoxia in senile dementia and other abiotrophies. *Brain*, **99**, 459–496.

Bowers, M. B. (1973) 5-Hydroxyindoleacetic acid (5-HIAA) and homovanillic acid (HVA) following probenecid in acute psychotic patients treated with phenothiazines. *Psychopharmacologia*, **28**, 309–318.

Bunney, B. S., and Aghajanian, G. K. (1975) The effect of antipsychotic drugs on the firing of dopaminergic neurons: A reappraisal, in, Sedvall, G., Uvnas, B., and Zotterman, Y. (eds.) *Antipsychotic Drugs: Pharmacodynamics and Pharmacokinetics*, Pergamon Press, New York, pp. 305–318.

Bunney, B. S., and Aghajanian, G. K. (1976) Dopaminergic influence in the basal ganglia: Evidence for striatonigral feedback regulation, in Yahr, M. (ed.), *The Basal Ganglia*, Raven Press, New York, pp. 249–267.

Bürki, H. R., Eichenberger, E., Sayers, A. C., and White, T. G. (1975) Clozapine and the dopamine hypothesis of schizophrenia: a critical appraisal. *Pharmakopsychiat.*, **8**, 115.

Burt, D. R., Creese, I., and Snyder, S. H. (1976) Properties of ^{3}H-haloperidol and ^{3}H-dopamine binding associated with dopamine receptors in calf brain membranes. *Mol. Pharmac.*, **12**, 800–812.

Burt, D. R., Creese, I., and Snyder, S. H. (1977) Antischizophrenic drugs: chronic treatment elevates dopamine receptor binding in brain. *Science*, **196**, 326–328.

Carenzi, A., Gillin, J. C., Guidotti, A., Schwartz, M. A., Trabucchi, M., and Wyatt, R. J. (1975) Dopamine-sensitive adenyl cyclase in human caudate nucleus. A study in control subjects and schizophrenic patients. *Arch. Gen. Psychiat.*, **32**, 1055–1059.

Chase, T. N. (1973) Biochemical and pharmacologic studies of monoamines in Huntington's chorea, in Barbeau, A., Chase, T. N., and Paulson, G. W. (eds.) *Advances in Neurology*, Raven Press, New York, vol. 1 pp. 533–542.

Cole, J. O., and Clyde, O. (1961) Extrapyramidal side effects and clinical response to the phenothiazines. *Rev. Canad. Biol.*, **20**, 565–574.

Connell, P. H. (1958) *Amphetamine Psychosis*, Oxford University Press, London.

Connor, J. D. (1970) Caudate nucleus neurones: correlation of the effects of substantia nigra stimulation with iontophoretic dopamine. *J. Physiol.*, **208**, 691.

Creese, I., Burt, D. R., and Snyder, S. H. (1976) Dopamine receptor binding predicts clinical and pharmacological potencies of antischizophrenic drugs. *Science*, **192**, 481–483.

Creese, I., and Iversen, S. D. (1975) The pharmacological and anatomical substrates of the amphetamine response in the rat. *Brain Res.*, **83**, 419–436.

Cross, A. J., Crow, T. J., Killpack, W. S., Longden, A., Owen, F., and Riley, G. J. (1978) The activities of brain dopamine-beta-hydroxylase and catechol-O-methyl transferase in schizophrenics and controls. *Psychopharmacology (Berlin)*, **59**, 117–121.

Crow, T. J., Baker, H. F., Cross, A. J., Joseph, M. H., Lofthouse, R., Longden, A., Owen, F., Riley, G. J., Glover, V., and Killpack, W. S. (1978a) Monoamine mechanisms in chronic schizophrenia: postmortem neurochemical findings. *Brit. J. Psychiat.*, **134**, 249–256.

Crow, T. J., Deakin, J. F. W., and Longden, A. (1977) The nucleus accumbens—possible site of antipsychotic action of neuroleptic drugs. *Psychol. Med.*, **7**, 213–221.

Crow, T. J., Owen, F., Cross, A. J., Lofthouse, R., and Longden, A. (1978). Brain biochemistry in schizophrenia. *Lancet*, i, 36–37.

Davies, P., and Maloney, A. J. F. (1976) Selective loss of central cholinergic neurons in Alzheimer's disease. *Lancet*, ii, 1403.

Ehringer, H., and Hornykiewicz, O. (1960) Verteilung von Noradrenalin und Dopamin (3-hydroxytyramin) im Gehirn des Menschen und ihr Verhalten bei Erkrankungen des extrapyramidalen Systems. *Klin. Wschr.*, **24**, 1236–1239.

Enna, S. J., Bennett, J. P., Burt, D. R., Creese, I., and Synder, S. H. (1976) Stereospecificity of interaction of neuroleptic drugs with neurotransmitters and correlation with clinical potency. *Nature*, **263**, 338–341.

Ettigi, P., Nair, N. P. V., Lal, S., Cervantes, P., and Guyda, H. (1976) Effect of apomorphine on growth hormone and prolactin secretion in schizophrenic patients, with or without oral dyskinesia, withdrawn from chronic neuroleptic therapy. *J. Neurol., Neurosurg., Psychiat.*, **39**, 870–876.

Falck, B., Hillarp, N.-Å., Thieme, G., and Torp, A. (1962) Fluorescence of catecholamines and related compounds condensed with formaldehyde. *J. Histochem. Cytochem.*, **10**, 348–356.

Farley, I. J., Price, K. S., McCullough, E., Deck, J. H. N., Hordynski, W., and Hornykiewicz, O. (1978) Norepinephrine in chronic paranoid schizophrenia: abovenormal levels in limbic forebrain. *Science*, **200**, 456–458.

Feltz, P., and DeChamplain, J. (1972) Enhanced sensitivity of caudate neurons to microiontophoretic injections of dopamine in 6-hydroxydopamine treated cats. *Brain Res.*, **43**, 601–605.

Foster, R., and Fyfe, C. A. (1966) Electron-donor-acceptor complex formation by compounds of biological interest. II. The association constants of various 4-dinitro-benzene-phenothiazine drug complexes. *Biochim. Biophys. Acta.*, **112**, 490.

Frantz, A. G., and Sachar, E. J. (1976) Effects of antipsychotic drugs on prolactin and growth hormone levels in man, in Sedvall, G., Uvnas, B., and Zotterman, Y. *Antipsychotic Drugs: Pharmacodynamics and Pharmacokinetics* Pergamon Press, Oxford, pp. 421–436.

Friedhoff, A. J., and van Winkle, E. (1962) Isolation and characterization of a compound from the urine of schizophrenics. *Nature*, **194**, 897–898.

Green, A. R., and Grahame-Smith, D. G. (1976a) Effects of drugs on the processes regulating the functional activity of brain 5-hydroxytryptamine. *Nature*, **260**, 487–491.

Green, A. R., and Grahame-Smith, D. G. (1976b) (−)-Propranolol inhibits the behavioural responses to increased 5-hydroxytryptamine in the central nervous system. *Nature*, **260**, 594–596.

Guth, P. S., and Spirtes, M. A. (1964) The phenothiazine tranquillizers: biochemical and biophysical actions. *Int. Rev. Neurobiol.*, **7**, 231.

Guyenet, P., Agid, Y., Javoy, F., Beaujouan, J. C., Rossier, J., and Glowinski, J. (1975) Effects of dopaminergic receptor agonists and antagonists on the activity of the neostriatal cholinergic system. *Brain Res.*, **84**, 227–236.

Hassler, R. (1938) Zur Pathologie der Paralysis agitans und des postencephalitischen Parkinsonismus. *J. Psychol. Neurol. (Leipzig)*, **48**, 387.

Hattori, T., Singh, V. K., McGeer, P. L., and McGeer, E. G. (1976) Immunohisto-chemical localization of choline acetyltransferase containing neostriatal neurons and their relationship with dopaminergic synapses. *Brain Res.*, **102**, 164–173.

Iversen, L. L. (1970) Neuronal uptake processes for amines and aminoacids, in, Costa, E., and Giacobini, E. (eds.) *Advances in Biochemical Psychopharmacology*, Raven Press, New York, p. 109.

Iversen, L. L. (1975) Dopamine receptors in brain. *Science*, **188**, 1084–1089.

Jacquet, Y. F., and Marks, N. (1976) The C-fragment of β-lipotropin: an endogenous neuroleptic or antipsychotogen? *Science*, **194**, 632–634.

Janowsky, D. S., Huey, L., Storms, L. H., and Judd, L. L. (1977) Methylphenidate hydrochloride effects on psychological tests in acute schizophrenic and non-psychotic patients. *Arch. Gen. Psychiat.*, **34**, 189–194.

Janssen, P. A. J., Niemegeers, C. J. E., and Schellekens, K. H. L. (1967) Is it possible to predict the clinical effects of neuroleptic drugs (major tranquillizers) from animal data? IV. *Arzneimittel-Forsch.*, **17**, 841–854.

Johnstone, E. C., Crow, T. J., and Mashiter, K. (1977) Anterior pituitary hormone secretion in chronic schizophrenia—an approach to neurohumoral mechanisms. *Psychol. Med.*, **7**, 223–228.

Kaufman, S., and Friedman, S., (1965) Dopamine-β-hydroxylase. *Pharmacol. Rev.*, **17**, 71.

Kebabian, J. W., and Calne, D. B. (1979) Multiple receptors for dopamine. *Nature*, **277**, 93–96.

Kety, S. S. (1967) Current biochemical approaches to schizophrenia. *New Eng. J. Med.*, **276**, 325–331.

Klawans, H. L., Goetz, C., and Westheimer, R. (1972) Pathophysiology of schizo-phrenia and the striatum. *Dis. Nerv. Syst.*, **33**, 711–719.

Klawans, H. L., and Weiner, W. J. (1974) The effect of d-amphetamine on chorei-form movement disorders. *Neurology (Minneap.)*, **24**, 312–318.

Ladinsky, H., Consolo, S., and Garattini, S. (1974) Increase in striatal acetyl-choline levels *in vivo* by piribedil, a new dopamine receptor stimulant. *Life Sci.*, **14**, 1251–1260.

Langer, G., Sachar, E. J., Gruen, P. H., and Halpern, F. S. (1977) Human prolactin responses to neuroleptic drugs correlate with antischizophrenic potency. *Nature*, **266**, 639–640.

Lee. T., Seeman, P., Tourtelotte, W. W., Farley, I., and Hornykiewicz, O. (1978) Binding of ^{3}H-neuroleptics and ^{3}H-apomorphine in schizophrenic brains. *Nature*, **274**, 897–900.

Levitt, M., Spector, S., Sjoerdsma, A., and Udenfriend, S. (1965) Elucidation of the rate-limiting step in norepinephrine biosynthesis in the perfused guinea-pig heart. *J. Pharmacol. exp. Ther.*, **148**, 1–8.

Leysen, J., and Laduron, P. (1977) Differential distribution of opiate and neuroleptic receptors and dopamine-sensitive adenylate cyclase in rat brain. *Life Sci.*, 20, 281–288.

Lightman, S. L., Spokes, E. G., Sagnella, G. A., Gordon, D., and Bird, E. D. (1979) Distribution of β-endorphin in normal and schizophrenic human brains. *Eur. J. Clin. Invest.*, 9, 377–379.

Lindvall, O., and Björklund, A. (1974) The organization of the ascending catecholamine neuron systems in the rat brain as revealed by the glyoxylic acid fluorescence method. *Acta physiol. scnad.*, Suppl. 412, 1–48.

Lloyd, K. G., Shibuta, M., Davidson, L., and Hornykiewicz, O. (1977) Chronic neuroleptic therapy: tolerance and GABA systems, in Costa, E., and Gessa, G. L. (eds.) *Advances in Biochemical Psychopharmacology* Raven Press, New York, vol. 16, pp. 409–415.

Matthysse, S. (1974) Dopamine and the pharmacology of schizophrenia: the state of the evidence. *J. Psychiat. Res.*, 11, 107–113.

Matthysse, S., and Lipinski, J. (1975) Biochemical aspects of schizophrenia. *Ann. Rev. Med.*, 26, 551–565.

McLennan, H., and York, D. H. (1967) The action of dopamine on neurons of the caudate nucleus. *J. Physiol.*, 189, 393–402.

Meltzer, H. Y., Sachar, E. J., and Frantz, A. G. (1974) Serum prolactin levels in unmedicated schizophrenic patients. *Arch. Gen. Psychiat.*, 31, 564–569.

Miller, R. J., and Hiley, C. R. (1974) Antimuscarinic properties of neuroleptics and drug-induced parkinsonism. *Nature*, 248, 596–597.

Nagatsu, T., Levitt, M., and Udenfriend, S. (1964) Tyrosine hydroxylase. The initial step in norepinephrine biosynthesis. *J. Biol. Chem.*, 239, 2910–2917.

O'Keefe, R., Sharman, D. F., and Vogt, M. (1970) Effects of drugs used in psychoses on cerebral dopamine metabolism. *Brit. J. Pharmacol.*, 38, 287–304.

Osmond, H., and Smythies, J. R. (1952) Schizophrenia. A new approach. *J. Ment. Sci.*, 98, 309–315.

Owen, F., Crow, T. J., Poulter, M., Cross, A. J., Longden, A., and Riley, G. J. (1978) Increased dopamine-receptor sensitivity in schizophrenia. *Lancet*, ii, 223–225.

Perry, E. K., Gibson, P. H., Blessed, G., Perry, R. H., and Tomlinson, B. E. (1977) Neurotransmitter enzyme abnormalities in senile dementia. *J. Neurol. Sci.*, 34, 247–265.

Perry, T. L., Buchanan, J., Kish, S. J., and Hansen, S. (1979) γ-Aminobutyric-acid deficiency in brain of schizophrenic patients. *Lancet*, i, 237–239.

Persson, T., and Roos, B.-E. (1969) Acid metabolites from monoamines in CSF of chronic schizophrenics. *Brit. J. Psychiat.*, 115, 95–98.

Pletscher, A. (1976) Biochemical and pharmacological aspects of Parkinson's syndrome: a short review, in, Birkmayer, W., and Hornykiewicz, O. (eds.) *Advances in Parkinsonism*, Editiones (Roche), Basle, pp. 21–36.

Poirier, L. J., and Sourkes, T. L. (1965) Influence of the substantia nigra on the catecholamine content of the striatum. *Brain*, 88, 181–192.

Pollin, W., Cardon, P. V., and Kety, S. S. (1961) Effect of amino acid feedings in schizophrenia patients with ipronazid. *Science*, 133, 104–105.

Post, R. M., Fink, E., Carpenter, W. T., and Goodwin, F. K. (1975) Cerebrospinal fluid amine metabolites in acute schizophrenia. *Arch. Gen. Psychiat.*, 32, 1063–1069.

Randrup, A., and Munkvad, I. (1965) Special antagonism of amphetamine-induced abnormal behaviour. Inhibition of stereotyped activity with increase of some normal activities. *Psychopharmacologia*, 7, 416–422.

Randrup, A., and Munkvad, I. (1966) On the role of catecholamines in the amphetamine excitatory response. *Nature*, 211, 540.

Randrup, A., and Munkvad, I. (1967) Stereotyped activities produced by amphetamine in several animal species and man. *Psychopharmacologia*, 11, 300–310.

Rimon, R., Roos, B.-E., Rakkolainen, V., and Alanen, Y. (1971) The content of 5-HIAA and HVA in the CSF of patients with acute schizophrenia. *J. Psychosom. Res.*, 15, 375–378.

Roberts, E. (1972) An hypothesis suggesting that there is a defect in the GABA system in schizophrenia. *Neurosci. Res. Prog. Bull.*, 10, 468–482.

Rotrosen, J., Angrist, B. M., Gershon, S., Sachar, E. J., and Halpern, F. S. (1976) Dopamine receptor alterations in schizophrenia: neuroendocrine evidence. *Psychopharmacology*, 51, 1–7.

Seeman, P., Lee, T., Chau-Wong, M., and Wong, K. (1976) Antipsychotic drug doses and neuroleptic/dopamine receptors. *Nature*, 261, 717–719.

Smythies, J. R. (1976) Recent progress in schizophrenia research, *Lancet*, ii., 136–139.

Snyder, S. H. (1973) Amphetamine psychosis: a 'model' schizophrenia mediated by catecholamines. *Am. J. Psychiat.*, 130, 61–67.

Snyder, S. H., Greenberg, D., and Yamamura, H. (1974) Antischizophrenic drugs and brain cholinergic receptors. Affinity for muscarinic sites predicts extrapyramidal effects. *Arch. Gen. Psychiat.*, 31, 58–61.

Spokes, E. G. (1979) An analysis of factors influencing measurements of dopamine, noradrenaline, glutamate decarboxylase, and choline acetylase in human post-mortem brain tissue. *Brain*, 102, 333–346.

Spokes, E. G. (1980) Neurochemical alterations in Huntington's chorea. A study of post-mortem brain tissue. *Brain*, 103, 179–210.

Spokes, E. G. S., Garrett, N. J., and Iversen, L. L. (1979) Differential effects of agonal status on measurements of GABA and glutamate decarboxylase in human post-mortem brain tissue from control and Huntington's chorea subjects. *J. Neurochem.*, 33, 773–778.

Spokes, E. G. S., Garrett, N. J., Rossor, M., and Iversen, L. L. (1980) GABA in control, schizophrenic and Huntington's chorea post-mortem brain. *J. Neurol. Sci.*, (submitted for publication).

Stawarz, R. J., Hill, H., Robinson, S. E., Setler, P., Dingell, J. V., and Sulser, F. (1975) On the significance of the increase in homovanillic acid (HVA) caused by antipsychotic drugs in corpus striatum and limbic forebrain. *Psychopharmacologia*, 43, 125–130.

Thudichum, H. (1884) *A treatise on the Chemical Constitution of the Brain.* Balliere, Tindall and Cox, London.

Ungerstedt, U. (1971) Stereotaxic mapping of the monoamine pathways in the rat brain. *Acta physiol. scand.*, Suppl. 367, 1–48.

Walters, J. R., and Roth, R. H. (1974) Dopaminergic neurons: drug-induced antagonism of the increase in tyrosine hydroxylase activity produced by cessation of impulse-flow. *J. Pharmacol. exp. Ther.*, 191, 82–91.

Weiner, N. (1970) Regulation of norepinephrine biosynthesis. *Ann. Rev. Pharmacol.*, 10, 273.

Weinshilboum, R. M., Thoa, N. B., Johnson, D. G., Kopin, I. J., and Axelrod, J. (1971) Proportional release of norepinephrine and dopamine-β-hydroxylase from sympathetic nerves. *Science*, 174, 1349–1351.

Westfall, T. C. (1974a) Effect of nicotine and other drugs on the release of ^{3}H-norepinephrine and ^{3}H-dopamine from rat brain slices. *Neuropharmacol.* 13, 693–700.

Westfall, T. C. (1974b) Effect of muscarinic agonists on the release of ^{3}H-norepinephrine and ^{3}H-dopamine and electrical stimulation from rat brain slices. *Life Sci.*, 14, 1641–1652.

Wise, C. D., and Stein, L. (1973) Dopamine-beta-hydroxylase deficits in the brain of schizophrenic patients. *Science*, **187**, 344–347.

Wyatt, R. J., Schwartz, M. A., Erdelyi, E., and Barchas, J. D. (1975) Dopamine-β-hydroxylase activity in brains of chronic schizophrenic patients. *Science*, **187**, 368–370.

Yorkston, N. J., Zaki, S. A., and Malik, M. K. (1974) Propanolol in the control of schizophrenic symptoms. *Brit. Med. J.*, **iv**, 633–635.

The Biochemistry of Psychiatric Disturbances
Edited by G. Curzon
© 1980 John Wiley & Sons Ltd.

CHAPTER 5

Drug Treatment of Schizophrenia and its Relationship to Disturbances of Dopaminergic Transmission

T. J. CROW

DIAGNOSTIC CRITERIA FOR SCHIZOPHRENIA

The psychoses as a group are distinguished from the neuroses and personality disorders by the presence of a disorder of perception, memory, or thinking such that the individual's 'grasp of reality' is impaired. It is generally held that the dysfunction in the psychoses represents a qualitative break with normality rather than a quantitative deviation such as may be present in neurotic and personality disorders. Among the psychoses the organic disorders (e.g. the dementias and confusional states) are conventionally distinguished from the functional psychoses by the presence of a disturbance of the capacity to acquire new information i.e. of learning. Such defects may also occur in some chronic schizophrenic illnesses (Crow and Mitchell, 1975; Johnstone et al., 1978a) but in general this is not the case in the acute psychoses. In the dementias, and possibly also in those chronic schizophrenic conditions where they are observed, learning defects may be associated with structural changes in the brain.

The schizophrenias and manic-depressive psychoses together constitute the group of functional psychoses. A rule of thumb is that in the affective disorders (manic-depressive psychoses) such disturbances of interpretation of reality (e.g. delusions, hallucinations) as are present can be understood as arising from a primary disturbance of mood. Thus delusions of poverty and disease are common in endogenous depression, and delusions of grandeur occur in hypomania. By contrast in schizophrenia, although affective disturbances are often present, there are psychopathological features which cannot be understood in this way. However, this criterion is too subjective to be reliable. Observers will differ in what they consider to be understandable. Moreover, it is unsatisfactory to arrive at a diagnosis only by a process of excluding other conditions. For this reason there has been considerable interest in the question of whether there are certain features whose presence can be used to establish a diagnosis of schizophrenia. The system which has attracted particular attention is Schneider's list of first rank (or nuclear) schizophrenic symptoms. According to Schneider (1957) the unequivocal presence of any one of these symptoms in the absence of organic brain disease is sufficient to establish an illness as schizophrenic. These symptoms are:

(1)   Hearing one's thoughts spoken aloud within one's head.
(2)   Hearing voices arguing.
(3)   Hearing voices that comment on what one is doing at the time.
(4)   Experiences of bodily influence.
(5)   Thought withdrawal, thought insertion, and other forms of thought interference.
(6)   Thought diffusion.
(7)   Delusional perception.
(8)   Everything in the spheres of feeling, drive, and volition which the patient experiences as imposed on him or influenced by others (Schneider, 1957).

These symptoms fall into three groups:
(a)   Auditory hallucinations of certain specific types (symptoms 1 to 3).
(b)   The conviction that subjective control of mental life is lost, and that movements, thoughts, feelings or volitions are in some way influenced from outside (symptoms 4, 5, 6 and 8).
(c)   Delusional perception (symptom 7)—the attribution of unusual significance or meaning to otherwise unexceptional perceptual experiences.

These symptoms can be reliably assessed and have been incorporated into the Present State Examination (Wing et al., 1974) a standardized psychiatric interview which aims to provide a systematic assessment of psychiatric state. Although these 'nuclear' symptoms by no means exhaust the manifestations of schizophrenia they serve to define a group of the most characteristically schizophrenic illnesses. The mechanisms by which they are produced are almost entirely obscure. However, it has been suggested (Frith, 1979) that some of these symptoms (e.g. the auditory hallucinations) could be understood if it were assumed that the patient had become aware of information processing which normally takes place below the level of consciousness.

According to this view the scope of the schizophrenic patient's conscious awareness has enlarged to include certain automatic and normally subconscious processes. The feature common to the second group of symptoms is that each is associated with intrusions into or interruptions of the stream of consciousness which are not recognized by the patient as arising from his own psychological activity. Delusional perception appears best explained as the inappropriate operation of a mechanism for attaching meaning or significance to perceptual experience.

It might be supposed that the neurochemical changes underlying these symptoms would be complex and they may well be so. Yet there is evidence that schizophrenic features in general, including first rank symptoms, can be increased or decreased by administration of relatively simple chemical substances. Symptoms can be made worse by the amphetamines, and better by the class of drugs known as neuroleptics.

THE AMPHETAMINE PSYCHOSIS

The similarity of the symptoms of the amphetamine psychosis to those of acute paranoid schizophrenia was emphasized by Connell (1958) who reported a series of cases from the Maudsley Hospital and pointed out that 'clouding of consciousness' (i.e. disorientation in time and space) the hallmark of the 'toxic' psychoses was generally absent in these cases and many typically schizophrenic features were present. Both in Connell's series and in that reported from Lexington, Kentucky by Ellinwood (1967) first rank symptoms were observed. Although the clinical features of the amphetamine psychosis and acute paranoid schizophrenia are both variable the view that without information on prior drug intake the two conditions cannot be distinguished appears well established.

It has been suggested that the symptoms of the amphetamine psychosis might be an idiosyncratic response in subjects predisposed to schizophrenia, or might be secondary to sleep deprivation. Both explanations are rendered unlikely by the findings of Griffith et al., (1972) that psychotic symptoms could be induced in most if not all volunteer subjects and that in some subjects these symptoms occurred without significant sleep deprivation.

Thus the pharmacological actions of the amphetamines are of particular interest. In their work on amphetamine-induced abnormal behaviours in various animal species Randrup and Munkvad (1967) established that the syndrome of stereotyped behaviours (which in rodents includes sniffing, licking, and gnawing behaviours) is dependent upon DA release. This conclusion is reinforced by the observation that these amphetamine-induced abnormal behaviours are abolished by lesions induced in central DAergic pathways by intracerebral injections of 6-OH-DA (Creese and Iversen, 1975).

By analogy with the animal experiments it is suggested that the symptoms of the amphetamine psychosis in man are due to increased DA release. There is evidence from a CSF study (Angrist et al., 1974) that DA turnover is increased after psychotogenic doses of amphetamine. Moreover, neuroleptic drugs which are known to block DA receptors both reverse the symptoms of the amphetamine psychosis (Gunne et al., 1972; Angrist et al., 1974) and selectively antagonize amphetamine-induced abnormal behaviours in animal experiments (Randrup and Munkvad, 1965).

On this basis it is argued that the amphetamine psychosis is a model for schizophrenia and that schizophrenic symptoms (i) may be due to increased DA release and (ii) may be diminished by the DA receptor blockade induced by neuroleptic drugs.

THE ACTION OF NEUROLEPTIC DRUGS

That neuroleptic drugs can induce symptoms resembling those of Parkinson's disease was apparent soon after the introduction of chlorpromazine. It was suggested by some (e.g. Deniker, 1960) that these neurological effects were related to the therapeutic action in schizophrenia. Although this was generally doubted because the correlation between the actions is not perfect, some drugs (e.g. thioridazine) causing parkinsonian side-effects less frequently than the reference drug chlorpromazine (National Institute of Mental Health, 1964), this theory has gained support in recent years. Newer groups of drugs with antipsychotic activity (e.g. the thioxanthenes and butyrophenones) also induce extrapyramidal effects and increasing knowledge of their pharmacological mechanism has suggested these to be closely related to the antipsychotic effect.

The work of Hornykiewicz (1973) established that DA was depleted in the brain of patients who died with Parkinson's disease. This is presumably a secondary consequence of degeneration of ascending DAergic pathways. Thus the symptoms of Parkinson's disease seem likely to be due to a failure of DAergic transmission. Although the drug reserpine (which can have parkinsonian effects) depletes central DA stores, neuroleptic drugs do not cause depletion. Instead they increase DA turnover (Carlsson and Lindqvist, 1963; O'Keefe et al., 1970) and it is suggested (Carlsson and Lindqvist, 1963) that this may be a secondary feedback response to DA receptor blockade.

With the development of in vitro assay systems for DA receptors the DA antagonist effects of neuroleptic drugs have been extensively studied. For example, it has been shown that the clinical potency of a range of drugs in schizophrenia correlates well with their ability to inhibit the DA-induced activation of adenylate cyclase activity in corpus striatum (Miller et al., 1974). There is also a highly significant correlation between therapeutic potency and activity in inhibiting the binding of haloperidol to striatal tissue (Creese et al., 1976; Seeman et al., 1976).

Some small variations in molecular structure can markedly affect DA receptor blocking activity. For example the drug promazine differs from chlorpromazine only in lacking a chlorine substituent on the 'a' ring (Figure 1) but is substantially less potent as a DA antagonist. It is also known to be less effective in the treatment of schizophrenia (Figure 2).

The finding that the stereoisomers of the thioxanthenes differ substantially in their DA antagonist potencies (Miller et al., 1974) made possible a rather stringent clinical test of the DA hypothesis. The two isomers of flupenthixol are both included in the widely used oral preparation of the drug but the α (cis-) isomer is more than 1,000 times more potent as a DA blocker than the β (trans-) isomer (Figures 3 and 4).

A clinical trial of the two isomers was therefore conducted (Johnstone et al., 1978b) to determine whether (as predicted by the hypothesis) antipsychotic activity was limited to the α-isomer. Patients were selected for the trial by a standardized interview (the Present State Examination) according to the presence of first rank

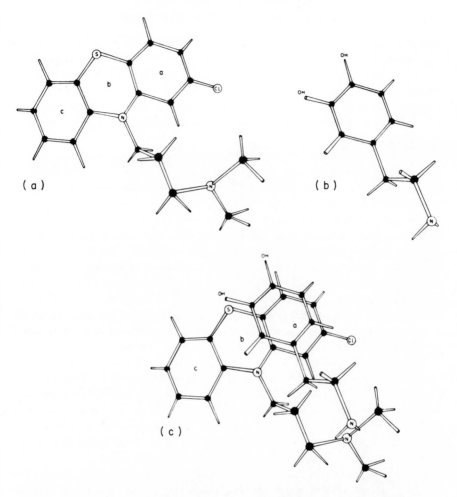

Figure 1. The stereochemical structures of chlorpromazine and DA and their possible relationship. Reproduced with permission from Horn and Snyder, 1971

(nuclear) schizophrenic symptoms and were allocated at random to α- or β-flupenthixol or placebo. According to the trial design they were permitted to receive extra chlorpromazine medication if this was made necessary by severe disturbance. Extra doses of chlorpromazine were treated as one of the dependent variables, the other being weekly ratings of clinical state. In either case the findings were the same. There were differences in favour of α-flupenthixol with respect to the β-isomer and placebo (Figure 5).

The differences were significant at the end of the third and fourth weeks. The findings are obviously compatible with the DA blockade hypothesis. Some other mechanisms of action (e.g. blockade of NA, opiate, and acetylcholine receptors)

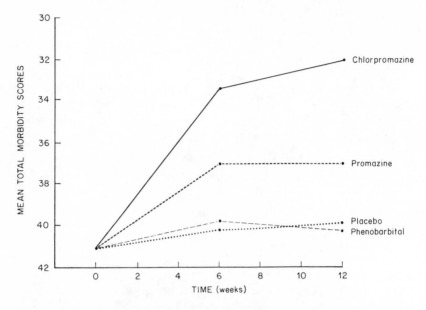

Figure 2. The therapeutic potency of promazine in comparison to chlorpromazine and to a barbiturate and placebo in the treatment of acute schizophrenia. Reproduced with permission from Klein and Davis (1969)

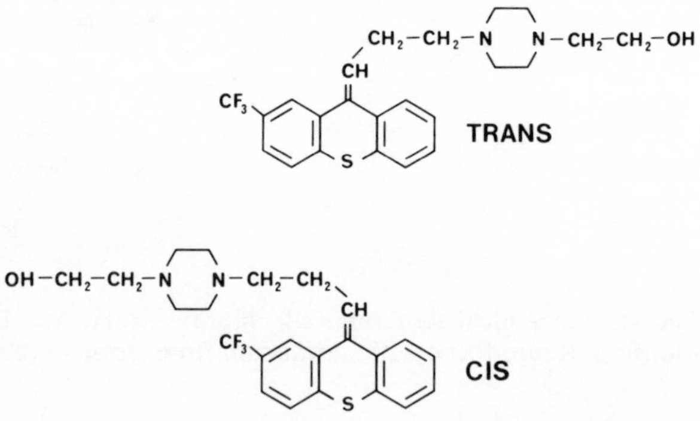

Figure 3. The α (*cis-*) and β (*trans-*) isomers of flupenthixol

can be ruled out since the two isomers are known to be of similar potency with respect to these receptors. The isomers do, however, differ from each other as antagonists of the 5-HT receptor (Enna *et al.*, 1976) the α-isomer being considerably
more potent. However, 5-HT antagonism is a poor predictor of antipsychotic activity for a range of psychotropic drugs (Bennett and Snyder, 1975) and the 5-HT antagonist cinanserin has been found to be without therapeutic activity in two clinical

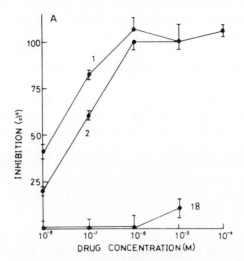

Figure 4. Inhibition of DA stimulation of striatal adenylate cyclase activity by α-flupenthixol (trace 1), the racemate of the two isomers (curve 2), and β-flupenthixol (curve 18). Reproduced with permission from Miller *et al.*, 1974

Flupenthixol trial

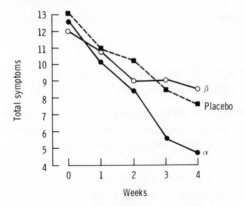

Figure 5. The effects of α- and β-flupenthixol and placebo on the symptoms of acute schizophrenia. Reproduced with permission from Johnstone *et al.*, 1978b)

trials. Therefore DA antagonism appears to be the only known pharmacological mechanism which will explain the therapeutic effect.

If both therapeutic effects and extrapyramidal effects are due to DA antagonism it remains to be explained why the relationship between the two is not constant, i.e. why drugs such as thioridazine have a lower than expected incidence of extra-pyramidal effects. The most plausible explanation advanced so far is that of Miller and Hiley (1974) who have shown that such drugs have relatively high anticholinergic activity. Thus these drugs may possess 'in-built' anti-parkinsonian activity in addition to their DA antagonist effects.

This implies that the extrapyramidal and antipsychotic effects cannot be occurring at the same sites in the brain as if this were so the antipsychotic, like the extrapyramidal effects of a drug like thioridazine would be reversed by the anticholinergic action. A comparison of the effects of three neuroleptic drugs, differing widely in incidence of extrapyramidal effects, on DA turnover in striatal and mesolimbic areas (i.e. nucleus accumbens) revealed that extrapyramidal effects correlated well with actions on DA in the striatum while the antipsychotic effects were more closely correlated with actions in the nucleus accumbens (Crow et al., 1977; Figure 6).

THE TIME COURSE OF THE ANTIPSYCHOTIC EFFECT

The trial of the isomers of flupenthixol demonstrated that the therapeutic effects attributable to drug therapy emerged rather slowly, becoming significant only at the end of week three of treatment. This time course can be contrasted with that of DA receptor blockade by measuring the rise in prolactin shown in patients on the α-isomer, since prolactin secretion is inhibited by DA. Comparison (Figure 7) reveals a delay of at least two weeks between DA receptor blockade and the change in clinical state attributable to the drug. Thus DA receptor blockade may be necessary to allow some other and slower process to take place which results in clinical change.

IS THERE AN UNDERLYING DISTURBANCE OF DAERGIC TRANSMISSION IN SCHIZOPHRENIA?

There have been a number of previous attempts to assess whether, as predicted by the DA hypothesis, DAergic transmission is increased in schizophrenia: (i) Bowers (1974) and Post et al. (1975) measured the DA metabolite HVA in CSF after probenecid administration. Neither study gave evidence of increased turnover of DA in unmedicated schizophrenic patients. (ii) Meltzer et al. (1974) and Johnstone et al. (1977) assessed serum prolactin in unmedicated acute and chronic schizophrenic patients respectively and found no evidence of the decrease which might be expected if DA release from the tuberoinfundibular system were tonically increased. (iii) Crow et al., (1976) described cases in which parkinsonism of both idiopathic and postencephalitic origin, coexisted with schizophrenic symptoms. The significance of these findings is enhanced by the demonstration (Farley et al., 1977) that in Parkinson's disease DA is as depleted in mesolimbic as in striatal areas. Thus the coexistence of schizophrenic and parkinsonian symptoms suggests that increased DA release is not essential for schizophrenic symptoms to appear.

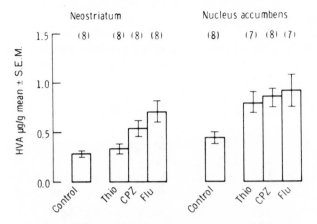

Figure 6. The effects of thioridazine (Thio), chlorpromazine (CPZ), and fluphenazine (Flu) on DA turnover
in two areas of rat brain. Reproduced with permission
from Crow *et al.*, 1977

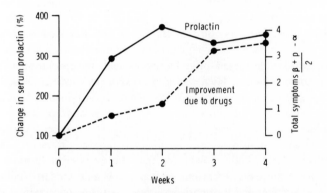

Figure 7. The time course of the antipsychotic effect in
schizophrenia (calculated as the difference between ratings
on active and inactive medication) compared to the time
course of the increase in prolactin secretion in patients
on α-flupenthixol. Reproduced with permission from
Cotes *et al.*, 1978

These findings provide little support for the view that DA release is increased in
schizophrenia. This conclusion is reinforced by the results of recent post-mortem
studies (Owen *et al.*, 1978), in which similar DA concentrations were found in
putamen and nucleus accumbens of brains of 19 schizophrenic patients and 19 controls. There was, however, a modest increase ($p < 0.05$) in the caudate nuclei of the
schizophrenics (Figure 8), but this, while similar in magnitude to that reported in

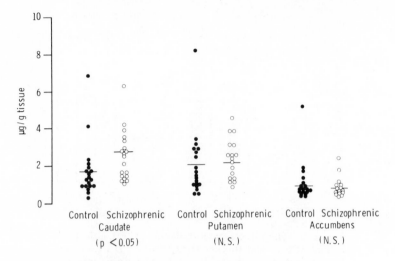

Figure 8. Concentrations of DA in post-mortem brain from patients with schizophrenia and controls. Reproduced with permission from Owen *et al*., 1978

other areas by other workers (Bird *et al*., 1977) does not seem to be a constant finding.

DA concentrations decrease rapidly following death and provide no index of turnover but the DA metabolites HVA and dihydroxyphenylacetic acid are better preserved and provide an indication of turnover. However, although the DA hypothesis predicts that HVA concentrations should be high this was not found. Indeed in caudate nucleus it was significantly low ($p < 0.02$). This may seem surprising since many patients had been on neuroleptics which might have been expected to increase DA turnover. However, there is evidence that the increase in turnover on acute administration disappears with chronic treatment. At all events the findings do not support the DA overactivity theory. Neither does the observation that dopacetic acid concentrations were similar in schizophrenics and controls in the DAergically-innervated areas examined.

A possible resolution of the paradox that DA receptor blockade is beneficial for schizophrenic patients and yet there is no evidence of DA neuron overactivity is that the defect lies not in the presynaptic neuron but in an increased sensitivity of the postsynaptic receptor (Bowers, 1974; Crow *et al*., 1976).

This possibility was tested (Owen *et al*., 1978) by applying the spiroperidol binding technique to post-mortem brain samples. At a ligand concentration of 0.8 nM a significant increase in binding was found in each of the three areas (Figure 10) and the values correlated well in individual patients between areas.

It is likely that in patients on neuroleptic medication some drug remains in the brain bound to membranes and can interfere with this estimation. Therefore

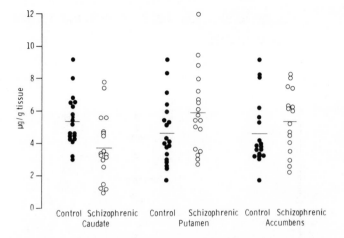

Figure 9. Concentrations of HVA in post-mortem brain from patients with schizophrenia and controls. Reproduced with permission from Owen *et al.*, 1978

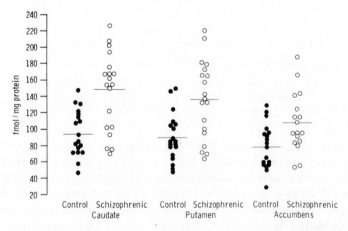

Figure 10. DA receptor concentrations (assessed with 0.8 nM spiroperidol as ligand) in post-mortem brain from schizophrenics and controls. Reproduced with permission from Owen *et al.*, 1978

maximum spiroperidol binding values, derived from a Scatchard analysis, are likely to be a better estimate of receptor density. Maximum binding was 100% greater in the schizophrenic patients than in the controls (Figure 11).

Significantly ($p < 0.05$) high values were found in two patients who apparently had never received neuroleptic medication, and also ($p < 0.01$) in a group of five patients (including the above two) who had been free of medication for the year

Maximum specific ^{3}H spiroperidol binding in preparations

of human caudate

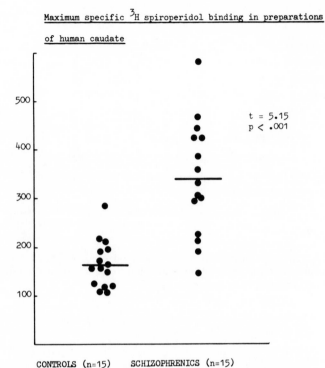

CONTROLS (n=15)   SCHIZOPHRENICS (n=15)

Figure 11. DA receptor concentrations (assessed as maximum spiroperidol binding capacities from a Scatchard analysis) in post-mortem brain from schizophrenics and controls. Reproduced with permission from Owen *et al.*, 1978

before death. Thus there is evidence that the increase in DA receptors observed in schizophrenic brain is not wholly due to previous neuroleptic medication. An increase in receptor numbers following neuroleptic treatment has been seen in animal experiments (Burt *et al.*, 1977) but is small (20-25%) compared with the increase we observed in schizophrenic brain and disappears within two to three weeks of discontinuing drug treatment. The increase in receptor numbers in schizophrenic brain, which has also been observed with haloperidol as ligand (Lee *et al.*, 1978b) is larger than that recently reported in the brains of patients dying with Parkinson's disease (Lee *et al.*, 1978a). Thus it seems possible that the mechanism by which the change in receptor numbers occurs in schizophrenia is different from that which is responsible for the increase following blockade or denervation of the receptor.

FUNCTIONS OF DA NEURONS

DAergic mechanisms have often been thought of as part of the extrapyramidal system and as being involved primarily in motor control. However, the following experiments suggest a more fundamental role for these neurons in behavioural regulation.

(i) After bilateral lesions of the ascending DA systems rats develop a syndrome of akinesia, aphagia, and adipsia which closely resembles the lateral hypothalamic syndrome (Ungerstedt, 1971). (ii) After unilateral lesions of DA neurons animals develop a syndrome of 'unilateral sensory inattention' in which they fail to respond to significant sensory stimuli in the contralateral sensory field (Marshall and Teitelbaum, 1974; Ungerstedt, 1974). (iii) With electrodes implanted on DA neurons rats can be trained to press a lever to deliver stimulation through the implanted electrode. This finding suggests that DA neurons function as a 'reward pathway' (Crow, 1972, 1977).

Together these findings suggest that DA neurons are involved in activating the organism's motor responses toward significant environmental stimuli. Thus in addition to being involved in the control of motor responses these pathways may be concerned in directing these responses toward the most appropriate features of the sensory environment. Although a precise account of the way in which this may occur is not available it seems possible that a disturbance in this mechanism might account for some of the features of schizophrenia.

SUMMARY

Typically schizophrenic symptoms can be induced in normal subjects and exacerbated in schizophrenic patients by amphetamine and can be ameliorated by neuroleptic drugs. Amphetamines and neuroleptics act respectively to enhance and diminish DAergic transmission. These facts have led to the DA hypothesis that schizophrenic symptoms are (i) due to increased DA release, and (ii) diminished by DA receptor blockade.

A clinical trial of the efficacy of the two isomers of flupenthixol in acute schizophrenia provided a test of the second component of this hypothesis. The findings were consistent with the view that DA receptor blockade is the only necessary component of the therapeutic effect, although the time course of action suggests that blockade may only gradually lead to this effect.

Post-mortem and other studies in schizophrenia provide no support for the view that there is overactivity of DA neurons in schizophrenia. However, there is evidence for an increase in numbers of DA receptors in two-thirds of the brains so far examined which cannot be explained by prior neuroleptic medication.

REFERENCES

Angrist, B., Lee, H. K., and Gershon, S. (1974) The antagonism of amphetamine-induced symptomatology by a neuroleptic. *Amer. J. Psychiat.*, **131**, 817–819.

Angrist, B., Sathananthan, G., Wilk, S., and Gershon, S. (1974) Amphetamine psychosis: behavioural and biochemical aspects. *J. Psychiat. Res.*, **11**, 13–23.

Bennett, J. P., and Snyder, S. H. (1975) Stereospecific binding of D-lysergic acid diethylamide (LSD) to brain membranes: relationship to serotonin receptors. *Brain Res.*, **94**, 523–544.

Bird, E. D., Spokes, E. G., Barnes, J. Mackay, A. V. P., Iversen, L. L., and Shepherd, M. (1977) Increased brain dopamine and reduced glutamic acid decarboxylase and choline acetyl transferase activity in schizophrenia and related psychoses. *Lancet*, **ii**, 1157–1159.

Bowers, M. B. (1974) Central dopamine turnover in schizophrenic syndromes. *Arch. Gen. Psychiat.*, **31**, 50–54.

Burt, D. R. Creese, I., and Snyder, S. H. (1977) Antischizophrenic drugs: chronic treatment elevates dopamine receptor binding in brain. *Science*, **196**, 326–328.

Carlsson, A., and Lindqvist, M. (1963) Effect of chlorpromazine and haloperidol on formation of 3-methoxy-tyramine and normetanephrine in mouse brain. *Acta Pharmacol. Toxicol.*, **20**, 140–144.

Connell, P. H. (1958) *Amphetamine Psychosis*, Maudsley Monograph No. 5, Chapman and Hall, London.

Cotes P. M., Crow, T. J., Johnstone, E. C., Bartlett, W., and Bourne, R. C. (1978) Neuroendocrine changes in acute schizophrenia as a function of clinical state and neuroleptic medication. *Psychol. Med.*, **8**, 657–665.

Creese, I., Burt, D. R., and Snyder, S. H. (1976) Dopamine receptor binding predicts clinical and pharmacological potencies of antischizophrenic drugs. *Science*, **192**, 481–483.

Creese, I., and Iversen, S. D. (1975) The pharmacological and anatomical substrates of the amphetamine response in the rat. *Brain. Res.*, **83**, 419–436.

Crow, T. J. (1972) Catecholamine-containing neurones and electrical self-stimulation. Part 1: a review of some data. *Psychol. Med.*, **2**, 414–421.

Crow, T. J. (1977) The neuroanatomy of intracranial self-stimulation: a general catecholamine hypothesis. *Neurosci. Res. Prog. Bull.*, **15**, 195–205.

Crow, T. J., Deakin, J. F. W., and Longden, A. (1977) The nucleus accumbens—a possible site of antipsychotic action of neuroleptic drugs? *Psychol. Med.*, **7**, 213–221.

Crow, T. J., Johnstone, E. C., and McClelland, H. A. (1976) The coincidence of schizophrenia and Parkinsonism: some neurochemical implications. *Psychol. Med.*, **6**, 227–233.

Crow, T. J., and Mitchell, W. S. (1975) Subjective age in chronic schizophrenia: evidence for a sub-group of patients with defective learning capacity? *Brit. J. Psychiat.*, **126**, 360–363.

Deniker, P. (1960) Experimental neurological syndromes and the new drug therapies in psychiatry. *Comp. Psychiat.*, **1**, 92–102.

Ellinwood, E. H. (1967) Amphetamine psychosis: I. Description of the individuals and process. *J. Nerv. Ment. Disease*, **144**, 274–283.

Enna, S. J., Bennett, J. P., Burt, D. R., Creese, I., and Snyder, S. H. (1976) Stereospecificity of interaction of neuroleptic drugs with neurotransmitters and correlation with clinical potency. *Nature (Lond.)*, **263**, 338–341.

Farley, I. J., Price, K. S., and Hornykiewicz, O. (1977) Dopamine in the limbic regions of the human brain: normal and abnormal, in Costa, E., and Gessa, G. L. (eds.) *Non-Striatal Dopamine*, Raven Press, New York, pp. 57–64.

Frith, C. D. (1979) Consciousness, information processing and schizophrenia. *Brit. J. Psychiat.*, **134**, 225–235.

Griffith, J. D., Cavanagh, J., Held, J., and Oates, J. A. (1972) Dextroamphetamine: evaluation of psychomimetic properties in man. *Arch. Gen. Psychiat.*, **26**, 97–100.

Gunne, L. M., Angaard, E., and Jonsson, L. E. (1972) Clinical trials with amphetamine blocking drugs. *Psychiat. Neurol. Neurochir. (Amsterdam)*, **75**, 225–226.

Horn, A. S., and Snyder, S. H. (1971) Chlorpromazine and dopamine: conformational similarities that correlate with the antischizophrenic activity of phenothiazine drugs. *Proc. Nat. Acad. Sci. USA*, **68**, 2325–2328.

Hornykiewicz, O. (1973) Dopamine in the basal ganglia. Its role and therapeutic implications. *Brit. Med. Bull.,* **29**, 172–178.

Johnstone, E. C., Crow, T. J., and Mashiter, K. (1977) Anterior pituitary hormone secretion in chronic schizophrenia—an approach to neurohumoural mechanisms. *Psychol. Med.* **7**, 223–228.

Johnstone, E. C., Crow, T. J., Frith, C. D., Stevens, M. Kreel, L., and Husband, J. (1978a) The dementia of dementia praecox. *Acta Psychiat. Scand.,* **57**, 305–324.

Johnstone, E. C., Crow, T. J., Frith, C. D., Carney, M. W. P., and Price, J. S. (1978b) Mechanism of the antipsychotic effect in the treatment of acute schizophrenia. *Lancet,* i, 848–857.

Klein, D. F., and Davis, J. M. (1969) *Diagnosis and Drug Treatment of Psychiatric Disorder,* Williams and Wilkins, Baltimore.

Lee, T., Seeman, P., Rajput, A., Farley, I. J., and Hornykiewicz, O. (1978a) Receptor basis for dopaminergic hypersensitivity in Parkinson's disease. *Nature,* **273**, 59–61.

Lee, T., Seeman, P., Tourtelotte, W. W., Farley, I. J., and Hornykiewicz, O. (1978b) Binding of ^{3}H-neuroleptics and ^{3}H-apomorphine in schizophrenic brains. *Nature,* **274**, 897–900.

Marshall, J. F., and Teitelbaum, P. (1974) Further analysis of sensory inattention following lateral hypothalamus damage in rats. *J. Comp. Physiol. Psychol.,* **86**, 375–395.

Meltzer, H. Y., Sachar, E. J., and Frantz, A. G. (1974) Serum prolactin levels in unmedicated schizophrenic patients. *Arch. Gen. Psychiat.,* **31**, 564–569.

Miller, R. J., and Hiley, C. R. (1974) Antimuscarinic properties of neuroleptics and drug-induced Parkinsonism. *Nature (Lond.),* **248**, 596–597.

Miller, R. J., Horn, A. S., and Iversen, L. L. (1974) The action of neuroleptic drugs on dopamine-stimulated adenosine cyclic 3′, 5′-monophosphate production in rat neostriatum and limbic forebrain. *Molec. Pharmacol.,* **10**, 759–766.

National Institute of Mental Health (1964) Psychopharmacology Service Center Collaborative Study Group: Phenothiazine treatment in acute schizophrenia. *Arch. Gen. Psychiat.,* **10**, 246–261.

O'Keefe, R., Sharman, D. F., and Vogt, M. (1970) Effect of drugs used in psychoses on cerebral dopamine metabolism. *Brit. J. Pharmacol.,* **38**, 287–304.

Owen, F., Cross, A. J., Crow, T. J., Longden, A., Poulter, M., and Riley, G. J. (1978) Increased dopamine receptor sensitivity in schizophrenia. *Lancet,* **ii**, 223.

Post, R. M., Fink, E., Carpenter, W. T., and Goodwin, F. K. (1975) Cerebrospinal fluid amine metabolites in acute schizophrenia. *Arch. Gen. Psychiat.,* **32**, 1013–1069.

Randrup, A., and Munkvad, I. (1965) Special antagonism of amphetamine-induced abnormal behaviours. *Psychopharmacologia,* **7**, 416–422.

Randrup, A., and Munkvad, I. (1967) Stereotyped activities produced by amphetamine in several animal species and man. *Psychopharmacologia,* **11**, 300–310.

Schneider, K. (1957) Primäre und sekundäre Symptome bei der Schizophrenie. *Fortsch. Neurol. Psychiat.,* **25**, 487–490.

Seeman, P., Lee, T., Chau-Wong, M., and Wong, K. (1976) Antipsychotic drug doses and neuroleptic/dopamine receptors. *Nature (Lond.),* **261**, 717–719.

Ungerstedt, U. (1971) Adipsia and aphagia after 6-hydroxydopamine induced degeneration of the nigrostriatal dopamine system. *Acta Physiol. Scand.,* **82, Supp.** **367**, 95–122.

Ungerstedt, U. (1974) Brain dopamine neurons and behaviour, in Schmitt, F. O., and Worden, F. G. (eds.) *The Neurosciences, Third Study Program,* MIT Press, Cambridge, Mass., pp. 695–703.

Wing, J. K., Cooper, J. E., and Sartorius, N. (1974) *Measurement and Classification of Psychiatric Symptoms,* Cambridge University Press, Cambridge.

The Biochemistry of Psychiatric Disturbances
Edited by G. Curzon
© 1980 John Wiley & Sons Ltd.

CHAPTER 6

Transmitter Metabolism and Behavioural Abnormalities in Liver Failure

G. CURZON

The other chapters in this volume deal with disorders in which psychiatric abnormalities—subjective disturbances of mood or of appraisal of information—are the major or the only clinical symptoms. Neurochemical research on these illnesses must therefore be particularly centred on human material. It is thus inevitably subject to severe restrictions and resultant difficulties of interpretation. Even when biochemical abnormalities associated with the psychiatric illness are detected we are often not sure whether they are of primary importance.

A somewhat different situation exists when studying major disorders of metabolism such as uraemia, diabetes, and liver failure which can lead to biochemical changes in the central nervous system and to disturbances of its function. Here, unlike in the purely psychiatric disorders, we can be reasonably confident about the nature of the primary disturbance and it is therefore relatively easy to obtain good animal models and use them to study associations between the metabolic disorders, transmitter metabolism and behaviour.

Animal models relevant to psychiatric disturbance do, of course, suffer from another source of uncertainty because disturbances corresponding to human psychiatric illness are largely inferred from abnormalities of motor activity. Such inferences may well be erroneous. The behavioural consequences of disturbed human brain chemistry, e.g. alcohol intoxication, often depend on cultural factors. It is even more likely that ethological differences between human and rat societies may lead to motor responses of quite different kinds to similar neurochemical changes.

In recent years, the pioneering work of Fischer's group on the effects of liver disease on brain transmitter metabolism has led to investigations in a number of laboratories, including our own, on how these changes occur and their responsibility for the central effects of liver disorders. Much of this work has been on animal models. It has been influenced by prevailing hypotheses on how extracerebral changes alter brain concentrations of certain amino acids which are transmitter precursors, and the effects of these changes on transmitter synthesis. It is of interest that when amino acid concentrations were determined in plasma, whole blood, cerebrospinal fluid and brain tissue of 45 patients with grade 3 or 4 coma due to fulminant hepatic failure (Record *et al.*, 1976) it was found that while most of the 19 amino acids determined were significantly increased in blood these increases were greatest for those concerned with neurotransmitter metabolism, i.e. tryptophan (free), tyrosine and phenylalanine. Furthermore, phenylalanine and tyrosine were among the amino acids which were significantly increased in cerebrospinal fluid and these amino acids and tryptophan were among the amino acids which were significantly increased in the brain. However, there was no correlation between the plasma concentrations of the amino acids and the severity of the hepatic coma. This agrees with work by Delafosse *et al.* (1977).

Because of the above results and similar findings by others (e.g. Fischer, 1975) particular attention has been paid to the increased brain concentrations of tryptophan and tyrosine in liver disease and their effects on 5-hydroxytryptamine (5-HT) and catecholamine metabolism.

NORMAL INFLUENCES ON BRAIN TRYPTOPHAN CONCENTRATION

This is a topic of some neurochemical interest because brain tryptophan hydroxylase, the rate-limiting enzyme for 5-HT synthesis, is normally unsaturated with its substrate tryptophan (Eccleston *et al.*, 1965; Friedman *et al.*, 1972; Gal *et al.*, 1978). Therefore the transport of tryptophan from blood to brain has an important role in the control of 5-HT synthesis. Alone among the amino acids a considerable fraction of tryptophan is present in plasma in a bound form—attached to albumin molecules (McMenamy, 1965). This binding is affected by plasma unesterified fatty acid (UFA), which is itself almost completely bound to albumin. At high UFA concentrations the percentage of plasma tryptophan in the free state is increased (Curzon *et al.*, 1973a, 1974).

There has been much controversy on whether binding to albumin alters the availability of plasma tryptophan to the brain or whether availability depends on competition for transport sites of plasma tryptophan (bound + free) with a group of amino acids (phenylalanine, tyrosine, valine, leucine, isoleucine), (reviewed in Curzon, 1979). When brain tryptophan uptake was measured from boluses of labelled tryptophan dissolved in buffer ± albumin and injected into the rat carotid the uptake of tryptophan by the brain was hardly affected by plasma binding (Yuwiler *et al.*, 1977). However, under more physiological conditions, i.e. when uptake was measured not from buffer but from the rat's own reinjected plasma, it was more dependent on free tryptophan concentration (Bloxam *et al.*, 1980). These experiments also suggested that about a third of the tryptophan influx occurred by a mechanism with which other amino acids did not compete. This agrees with Mans *et al.* (1979a) who, using a similar method found that tryptophan transport into the rat brain was explicable by two kinetically distinct mechanisms: (a) a low capacity system obeying Michaelis–Menten kinetics and competed for by large neutral amino acids, and (b) an apparently unsaturatable system, not competed for by other amino acids and accounting for 40% of tryptophan influx under normal conditions.

TRYPTOPHAN AND BRAIN 5-HT METABOLISM IN HUMAN LIVER DISEASE

Some years ago, in collaboration with the Liver Unit at King's College Hospital, we found that CSF from patients with liver disease and encephalopathy contained high concentrations of 5-hydroxyindoleacetic acid (5-HIAA) and homovanillic acid (HVA) the terminal metabolites of 5-HT and dopamine (DA) (Table 1). These results suggested that increased turnover of these transmitters might be occurring in the brain during liver failure. More direct evidence was obtained from autopsy specimens taken 1 h after death (Record *et al.*, 1976). Tryptophan concentrations in frontal lobe from subjects who had died of fulminant hepatic failure was higher than in similar material from patients dying without evidence of liver disease (Table 2). The 5-HT metabolite 5-HIAA was also increased. These brain changes were not merely a consequence of increased plasma total tryptophan as although values were widely scattered the mean concentration was normal. However, plasma free tryptophan and UFA were both strikingly raised.

Related findings have been obtained by others. In particular, Ono *et al.*, (1978) report increased CSF tryptophan in patients with liver disease. Tryptophan values for comatose patients were significantly higher than for cirrhotics but other CSF amino acids (phenylalanine, tyrosine, methionine) were comparably increased in both groups. The CSF tryptophan changes were explicable by increases of plasma UFA and decreases of albumin concentrations rather than by the moderate changes of competing amino acid concentrations. Furthermore, Jellinger *et al.*, (1977, 1978) found increased brain tryptophan concentrations in hepatic coma in agreement with our own more limited results. Brain 5-HT and 5-HIAA were also increased in hepatic and other metabolic comas with particularly high values in the brainstem tegmentum and parts of the limbic system. In liver cirrhosis without coma brain 5-HT was normal and although tryptophan and 5-HIAA were elevated in the brainstem these increases were relatively negligible.

Table 1. Lumbar CSF HVA and 5-HIAA in fulminant hepatic encephalopathy and related disorders

	HVA (ng ml^{-1})	5-HIAA (ng ml^{-1})
Encephalopathy from fulminant hepatic failure	123 ± 120*(16)	86 ± 81*(18)
Encephalopathy complicating chronic liver disease	147 ± 113*(11)	78 ± 63*(10)
All patients with hepatic encephalopathy	129 ± 112*(27)	80 ± 53*(28)
Liver disease without encephalopathy	23 ± 13 (14)	27 ± 4 (3)
Miscellaneous neurological disorders	38 ± 13 (23)	22 ± 10 (23)

Number of patients in brackets. Values given ± S.D.
*Significantly greater than in patients with miscellaneous neurological disorders. Data from Knell *et al.* (1974)

Table 2. Plasma and brain indoles in fulminant hepatic failure

| | Plasma UFA (mEq l^{-1}) | Plasma Tryptophan (μg ml^{-1}) | | Brain Indoles (μg g^{-1} wet wt) | | |
		Total	Free	Tryptophan	5-HT	5-HIAA
Controls	0.40 ± 0.16 (10)	10.70 ± 1.07 (10)	0.80 ± 0.10 (10)	7.70 ± 1.59 (5)	0.21 ± 0.04 (5)	0.30 ± 0.05 (5)
Patients	1.46 ± 1.06 (9)†	11.63 ± 0.96 (22)	5.25 ± 0.70 (22)‡	18.49 ± 4.75 (13)*	0.30 ± 0.02 (13)	0.58 ± 0.06 (13)*

Plasma samples were taken when patients were in coma. Brain was frontal cortex taken within 1 h of death. Numbers of subjects in brackets. Values given ± S.E.M.
Differences from controls: *$p < 0.05$; †$p < 0.02$; ‡$p < 0.01$.
Data from Record et al. (1976) except for UFA values which are from Knell et al. (1974)

However, in work from Sourkes laboratory (1978) it was found that although CSF tryptophan was high in patients with hepatic cirrhosis its concentration was not significantly greater in patients with coma. Furthermore, although CSF 5-HIAA was raised in the latter group this seemed largely to reflect impaired transport as values were not significantly different from those of controls if both groups were given probenecid to block egress of 5-HIAA from the CSF.

The above findings in general and various drug experiments (Curzon and Knott, 1974) suggested that increased brain tryptophan and 5-HT metabolism in liver disease and in particular in hepatic coma were due to elevation of plasma free tryptophan. Munro *et al.* (1975) put forward a different explanation, according to which increased plasma insulin in liver failure decreases plasma concentrations of branched chain amino acids which compete with tryptophan for transport into the brain. This has some plausibility as plasma insulin concentration rises much more markedly after meals in cirrhotic than in normal subjects (Fernstrom *et al.*, 1978) and experiments in rabbits show that comparable insulin changes double the rate of entry of tryptophan into the brain (Daniel *et al.*, 1979).

The experiments described below on animal models of liver failure on the whole substantiate the hypothesis that plasma free tryptophan is an important influence on brain tryptophan concentration in liver failure and in normal states. However, this alone does not completely explain the findings and (as will be shown) disturbances of various other mechanisms affecting tryptophan transport also contribute to the brain changes.

TRYPTOPHAN AND BRAIN 5-HT METABOLISM IN ANIMALS WITH EXPERIMENTAL LIVER DISTURBANCE

In our first experiments on acute liver failure (Curzon *et al.*, 1973b) hepatic devascularization was obtained in pigs by porto-caval anastomosis followed by ligation of the hepatic artery. Sham operated animals recovered rapidly from the anaesthetic and appeared normal 1 h after operation, but the pigs with devascularized livers began to hyperventilate after 1–2 h. After 3 h, movements became unco-ordinated and the animals staggered and fell when trying to walk. By 5 h they did not respond to normally pain-provoking stimuli and some had epileptic fits. Blood pressure fell progressively. Seven out of nine devascularized pigs died 5.5–8.5 h after operation and the remaining two were killed at 8.25 and 9.5 h when their blood pressure fell below 40 mm Hg.

After devascularization there was a downward trend of plasma total tryptophan concentration in three out of four pigs but all four animals showed a marked increase in plasma free tryptophan, presumably due to the rise of plasma UFA which also occurred. The increase of plasma free tryptophan was associated with a rise of brain tryptophan which seemed to increase 5-HT turnover as indicated by raised 5-HIAA. Comparable findings are reported in rats with experimental acute liver failure (Cummings *et al.*, 1976a; Mans *et al.*, 1979b). In our work on pigs, changes of plasma concentrations of amino acids competing with tryptophan for transport to the brain were negligible (Buxton *et al.*, 1974) and Mans *et al.*, (1979b) found that competing amino acid concentrations were *increased* so that (if anything) they would have tended to impair tryptophan transport. It is clear, therefore, that such plasma amino acid changes did not contribute to the increased brain tryptophan and 5-HT metabolism in these experiments.

Rather similar metabolic changes were also found in rats with acute hepatic necrosis obtained by carbon tetrachloride injection (Knott and Curzon, 1975). Some 48 h after injection there were large increases of plasma UFA and free (but not total) tryptophan. Brain, liver, and muscle tryptophan concentrations increased significantly with percentage changes in the order: brain > liver > muscle > kidney. The increased brain tryptophan was associated with a small but significant increase of 5-HT and a larger increase of 5-HIAA.

In these acute experiments, brain tryptophan and plasma free tryptophan values for the control and treated groups taken together could be related by a single regression line. This was not the case when brain tryptophan was plotted against plasma *total* tryptophan.

While hepatic devascularization is rapidly fatal, chronic liver defect with survival for months can be produced in rats by porto-caval anastomosis without hepatic artery ligation. Brain tryptophan, 5-HT, and 5-HIAA are all consistently increased (Baldessarini and Fischer, 1973). Relationships between plasma and brain tryptophan obtained in our own work on anastomosed rats is illustrated in Figure 1. In these experiments the animals were given L-tryptophan (20 mg kg^{-1}) or saline seven weeks after operation and killed 90 min later. The figure shows correlation coefficients between brain regional tryptophan concentrations and both plasma free and plasma total tryptophan concentrations. Correlations with free tryptophan for the larger regions were in general positive and significant. Corresponding correlations for smaller regions (hypothalamus, hippocampus, and striatum) were less striking (possibly for methodological reasons) but with one exception they were positive and often significant. The only positive and significant correlation with total plasma tryptophan was for the hypothalamus of sham operated rats. Thus the results, in general, strongly suggest relationship between plasma free tryptophan and brain tryptophan concentrations. However, Figure 2 shows that this alone does not explain the high brain tryptophan concentration in the anastomosed rats. It gives the regression lines for the relationships between midbrain tryptophan and plasma free tryptophan concentrations. The lines for the saline and tryptophan treated sham operated groups are similar with respect to both slope and intercept. The lines for the corresponding anastomosed groups are steeper (consistent with more effective tryptophan uptake by the brain) but again are similar for both groups.

The above results suggest that the systems transporting tryptophan are altered by porto-caval anastomosis so that the amino acid is transferred more effectively to the brain. Similar findings have been reported by others (Cummings *et al.*, 1976; Mans *et al.*, 1976b). The increased transport is not specific to tryptophan but occurs

CORRELATION COEFFICIENTS

BRAIN TP v. PLASMA FREE TP
        v. PLASMA TOTAL TP

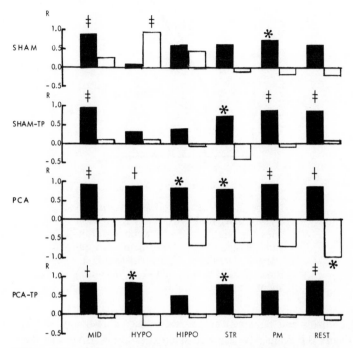

Figure 1.   Portocaval anastomosis and tryptophan administration. Correlation coefficients (R) between brain regional
tryptophan and plasma tryptophan concentrations. Saline or L-
tryptophan (20 mg kg^{-1}) injected i.p. and rats killed 90 min
later. From D. L. Bloxam, G. Curzon, and B. D. Kantamaneni,
unpublished work. *$p < 0.05$; †$p < 0.02$; ‡ $p < 0.01$; N = 6-7

also for the other large neutral amino acids (Bloxam and Curzon, 1978; James *et al.*,
1978). More recently, Mans *et al.*, (1979b) reported evidence that during acute
hepatic failure (hepatic artery ligation 65 h after porto-caval shunt) tryptophan influx
to the rat brain via both the low and high capacity systems (see page 90) is enhanced.
The contribution by the high capacity system is increased so that it accounts for 75%
of all tryptophan transport from plasma to brain. As this system is not competed
for by the large neutral amino acids the results of Mans *et al.*, (1979a) may explain
why brain tryptophan is increased in liver failure even when plasma concentrations
of these amino acids are increased.

In an investigation of the time course of changes of rat brain tryptophan metabolism after anastomosis (Bloxam and Curzon, 1978), it was found that brain tryptophan concentration 24 h after operation was already twice as high as in sham

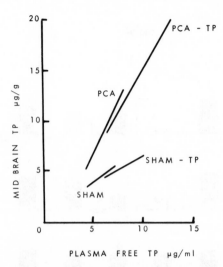

Figure 2.   Portocaval anastomosis and tryptophan administration. Regression lines for relationships between midbrain and plasma free tryptophan concentrations. Details as Figure 1. From D. L. ' Bloxam, G. Curzon, and B. D. Kantamaneni, unpublished work

operated controls and remained comparably raised throughout the 21 day study period (Figure 3). Brain 5-HT showed small rises but 5-HIAA was about 75% elevated throughout. Previous work in which regional 5-HT changes were measured three weeks after chronic anastomosis (Curzon *et al.*, 1975) showed significant increases in midbrain, pons ± medulla and hypothalamus but not in the hippocampus. Another study (Cummings *et al.*, 1976b) made four weeks after operation showed very similar 5-HT changes in midbrain and pons + medulla but concentrations in other regions (cortex, striatum, cerebellum and hypothalamus) were not significantly increased.

In the work of Bloxam and Curzon (1978) the brain indole increases occurred together with small increases of plasma total tryptophan (about 20%) and proportionately larger ones of free tryptophan (about 60%). As before, brain tryptophan correlated positively with plasma free tryptophan for both control and test groups. Also as before, increased plasma free tryptophan only partly explained the brain changes.

The increased ratios of brain tryptophan to plasma free tryptophan are not explained by the insulin hypothesis of Munro *et al.* (1975) as plasma insulin did not rise appreciably until more than four days after operation (Figure 4) but the brain: plasma ratios for tryptophan were already maximal 24 h after operation. The altered ratios are also not explained by an increased ratio of insulin to glucagon.

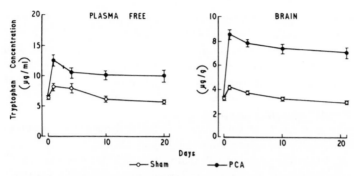

Figure 3.   Plasma free and brain tryptophan concentrations at different times after portocaval anastomosis (●) or sham operation (○), 7–10 rats per group. Bars indicate S.E.M. Reproduced from Bloxam and Curzon, 1978 with permission of *Journal of Neurochemistry*

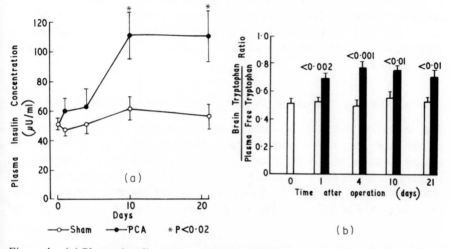

Figure 4.   (a) Plasma insulin concentrations at different times after portocaval anastomosis (●) or sham operation (○). (b) Ratio of brain tryptophan to plasma free tryptophan after portocaval anastomosis ■ or sham operation ▭. Other details as Figure 3. Reproduced from Bloxam and Curzon, 1978 with permission of *Journal of Neurochemistry*

This ratio may be physiologically more important than insulin levels (Unger, 1971; Parrilla *et al.*, 1974). However, it was not increased by anastomosis but was rapidly and substantially reduced and remained low. Similar results have been obtained in acute experimental liver failure (Mans *et al.*, 1979b).

In the study of Bloxam and Curzon (1978) plasma free but not total tryptophan had predictive value for brain tryptophan. This conclusion was essentially unaltered if the competitive effects of other amino acids on tryptophan transport were allowed for by the method of Pardridge and Oldendorf (1975).

In general, our experiments on the effects of anastomosis showed positive and significant correlations between plasma UFA, plasma free tryptophan and brain tryptophan. However, increases of UFA after anastomosis vary considerably from experiment to experiment (Curzon *et al.*, 1975; Cummings *et al.*, 1976b) and may depend on environmental conditions. Plasma UFA is well known to rise as a result of stress (Taggart and Carruthers, 1971) or sympathetic activity (Robison *et al.*, 1971) which can thus increase plasma free tryptophan and brain tryptophan (Knott and Curzon, 1972; Knott *et al.*, 1977; Gentil *et al.*, 1977). Results in Table 3 suggest that lipolytic responses to environmental stimuli are magnified in anastomosed rats, perhaps as a result of sympathetic abnormalities (Fischer *et al.*, 1976a) or defective hepatic UFA removal. Thus, while mean UFA values were invariably larger than those of identically treated sham-operated rats the differences between the values were small when the animals were taken from their home cages, somewhat larger after 95 min in an open field, and still larger and highly significant after 35 min intermittent foot shock. These findings suggest that not only does liver damage increase brain tryptophan for the reasons discussed but also that stress can increase brain tryptophan and hence 5-HT synthesis more markedly in anastomosed rats than in normal animals.

INFLUENCE OF TYROSINE ON BRAIN CATECHOLAMINE METABOLISM

Indications that brain 5-HT synthesis is affected by precursor availability within the physiological range have encouraged study of similar relationships for other transmitters. Smith *et al.*, (1977) report that rat brain catecholamine synthesis is not greatly affected by giving tyrosine, and our own results on human material are consistent with this (Curzon *et al.*, 1976) in so far as these relationships can be investigated in man. The lack of relationship does not, however, necessarily imply total

Table 3. Plasma unesterified fatty acid (UFA) concentration of rats with portocaval anastomosis (PCA)

Conditions	UFA (mEq l^{-1}) Sham operated	PCA
Home cage†	0.22 ± 0.11 (10)	0.28 ± 0.20 (12)
Open field 95 min‡	0.51 ± 0.25 (7)	0.83 ± 0.45 (6)
Intermittent foot shock 35 min‡	0.32 ± 0.13 (5)	0.92 ± 0.02 (3)*

Values are means ± S.D. Numbers of rats in brackets. Difference from sham-operated group, *$p < 0.001$
†Details in Curzon *et al.* (1975)
‡Details in Tricklebank *et al.* (1978)

insensitivity to increased tyrosine availability. It appears that DA synthesis increases initially when tyrosine is given but that this is opposed by feedback changes generated from postsynaptic receptors. Thus, if these receptors are blocked by haloperidol, then increasing brain tyrosine does increase DA turnover (Wurtman and Fernstrom, 1976) although as the receptors are blocked this is presumably of little functional importance. Tyrosine also can increase brain concentrations of the NA and adrenaline metabolite 3-methoxy 4-hydroxyphenylglycol sulphate (Gibson and Wurtman, 1978) which may indicate increased release of one or both parent transmitters (Sved et al., 1979).

A pathway of tyrosine metabolism of particular interest in liver failure is the route to octopamine. This is synthesized by the side chain hydroxylation of tyramine which is produced in considerable amount by decarboxylation of tyrosine in the gut and is normally destroyed in the liver. Octopamine is also formed in brain and other tissues (Molinoff and Buck, 1976) and its synthesis therein is increased if tyrosine or phenylalanine are injected (Harmer and Horn, 1976).

TYROSINE METABOLISM IN HUMAN LIVER DISEASE

Plasma tyrosine concentration is considerably increased in human liver failure with encephalopathy (Iber et al., 1957; Record et al., 1976; Delafosse et al., 1977) and brain tyrosine is also increased (Record et al., 1976). However, there is no evidence that this leads to increased catecholamine sythesis. Indeed, Jellinger et al. (1978) found slightly decreased DA concentrations in various brain regions of patients who had died with hepatic coma.

Fischer and Baldessarini (1971) noted that urinary excretion of octopamine was increased in patients with hepatic encephalopathy and Rossi-Fanelli et al. (1976) showed that this change correlated with the severity of hepatic encephalopathy. As antibiotics confer some benefit (Dodsworth et al., 1973) these findings suggest that octopamine (or other substances such as phenylethanolamine which are synthesized through gut bacterial action) have toxic effects in liver disease. Fischer and Baldessarini (1971) suggested that such effects result from the accumulation of octopamine in catecholamine neurons and consequent displacement of peripheral and central catecholamines from presynaptic sites. Findings in laboratory animals (see below) support this hypothesis.

BRAIN CATECHOLAMINE METABOLISM IN ANIMALS
WITH EXPERIMENTAL LIVER DISTURBANCE

Large increases of brain tyrosine occur in laboratory animals after porto-caval anastomosis (Bloxam and Curzon, 1978; Curzon et al., 1975; Mans et al., 1979b; Smith et al., 1978) and are only partly explained by the more moderate rises of plasma tyrosine concentration or by the decreased concentrations of amino acids competing for transport to the brain which are noted in some studies. Increased activity of the blood-brain neutral amino acid transport system is involved in the above brain changes (James et al., 1978, 1979).

Striatal DA concentration did not alter significantly in anastomosed rats (Curzon et al., 1975). Also, evidence is against abnormalities of catecholamine receptors as Laursen et al. (1977) found that NA or DA stimulated striatal adenylate cyclase activities were unaffected. Brain octopamine, however, rose up to five-fold (James et al., 1976) and correlated significantly with the rise of brain tyrosine. These biochemical changes both correlated significantly and negatively with the ratio of liver weight to bodyweight—an index of impaired liver function in anastomosed rats. As neither octopamine nor its precursor tyramine readily cross the blood-brain barrier these results suggest that brain octopamine increased as a result of the brain tyrosine changes. However, in view of evidence of alterations of blood-brain transport systems after liver shunt (Cremer et al., 1977; James et al., 1978; Mans et al., 1979a) passage of plasma octopamine to the brain cannot be excluded.

A study of plasma and CSF changes in dogs after portocaval anastomosis (Smith et al., 1978) is of particular interest. Unlike similarly operated rats, these animals after 4-18 weeks developed marked clinical features characteristic of hepatic encephalopathy—hypersalivation, ataxia, flapping tremor, somnolence, and finally coma. The development of clinical signs correlated well with increases of plasma and CSF tryptophan, tyrosine, phenylalanine, octopamine, and phenylethanolamine.

When aromatic amino acid concentrations increase in the brain then synthesis of octopamine, phenylethanolamine and other trace amines dependent on aromatic amino acid decarboxylase activity for their synthesis increase much more markedly than do the catecholamines. This is because the decarboxylase is normally much less saturated with amino acid substrate than is tyrosine hydroxylase, the rate-limiting enzyme for catecholamine synthesis. James et al. (1976) point out that this differential dependence on precursor concentration leads to an increased octopamine to NA ratio as brain tyrosine rises. Therefore, while octopamine may normally be

Table 4. Rat brain octopamine (OCT) and noradrenaline (NA) concentrations in experimental
hepatic coma

Rats	OCT $(ng\ g^{-1})$	NA $(ng\ g^{-1})$
Normal	3.8	300
Acute Shunt*		
Not comatose	6.4	270
Coma 9 h	11.3	180
Moribund	13.4	140

*Portocaval anastomosis and hepatic artery ligation
At least seven rats per group. Data from Dodsworth et
al. (1974)

unimportant it may appreciably alter both central and peripheral adrenergic function through the 'false neurotransmitter' action of octopamine when hepatic control over tyrosine disposal is defective.

The depletion of brain NA which occurs in acute experimental hepatic coma (Dodsworth et al., 1974) is shown in Table 4. After hepatic devascularization the animals gradually became increasingly comatose and this was associated with an increase of octopamine and decrease of NA concentrations in the brain. Serum octopamine and heart NA concentrations rose and fell roughly in parallel with their changes in the brain.

The relationships between the changes of aromatic amino acid disposition and brain transmitter metabolism which occur in liver failure are summarized in Figure 5.

OTHER NEUROCHEMICAL CHANGES IN LIVER DISTURBANCE

Chronic portocaval anastomosis increased brain ammonia and glutamine but not glutamic acid. When the hepatic artery was also ligated (acute hepatic coma) then the glutamine change was somewhat greater and ammonia concentrations rose manyfold. There was also a moderate but significant increase of brain GABA (Mans et al., 1979b), although this may possibly have reflected post-mortem changes (Mans, 1979).

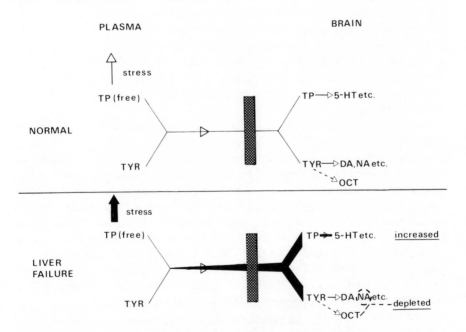

Figure 5.   Effect of experimental liver failure on relationships between plasma and brain aromatic amino acid concentrations and resultant transmitter changes

THE ROLE OF TRANSMITTER CHANGES IN HEPATIC ENCEPHALOPATHY

In human hepatic encephalopathy a spectrum of changes indicative of impaired brain function occurs commencing with changes of mood and signs of intellectual impairment, leading to confusion, slurred speech, drowsiness, hypersomnia, stupor, and coma as the condition worsens (Sherlock, 1968; Plum and Hindfelt, 1976). Some of these changes may also appear in less severe liver disease (Elithorn et al., 1975). Various clinical observations suggest that transmitter changes play some part in the development of these central symptoms. For example, Ogihara et al. (1966) found that a dog with portocaval anastomosis showed neurological changes if fed with tryptophan but not with other amino acids. Also, Condon (1971) showed that the survival of such animals was decreased if they were fed on diets containing large amounts of tryptophan and other aromatic amino acids. Furthermore, Hirayama (1971) noted that some patients with liver cirrhosis suffered from drowsiness, dizziness, and disturbances of gait after an oral tryptophan load, while similarly treated normal subjects showed milder effects.

Rats with portocaval anastomosis are not comatose and though they are reported to be less active than sham-operated rats Homlin and Siesjo (1974) reported that they reacted normally to auditory or tactile simuli. However, these conclusions were not based on systematic behavioural study. Subsequently, Monmaur et al. (1976) reported that anastomosed rats (like patients with hepatic encephalopathy) had disturbed sleep patterns with decreases of both slow wave and paradoxical sleep. Also, when cortical awakening was investigated by electrical stimulation of the brainstem reticular formation, then anastomosed animals were found to be awakened by an abnormally low stimulus voltage (Beaubernard et al., 1977). The type of sleep disturbance indicated is not obviously related to the increased brain 5-HT as drugs or procedures which increase or decrease this increase or decrease sleep respectively (Jouvet, 1968; Koella, 1974).

In another behavioural study of rats after portocaval anastomosis, Tricklebank et al. (1978) found a number of behavioural abnormalities. Motor activity in the home cage was slightly but not significantly increased during the day but was significantly decreased at night (Figure 6(a))—when rats are most active. Anastomosed animals were less active than sham-operated rats when placed in an open field under white light during their active period (Figure 6(b)). Furthermore, normal rats showed a similar decrease of activity if given a moderate dose of tryptophan. This latter finding confirms earlier work by Taylor (1976). However, its relevance to the central tryptophan and 5-HT changes in liver failure is unclear as although the effect of tryptophan can be blocked by 5-HT antagonists it is also prevented by a peripheral decarboxylase inhibitor (Tricklebank et al., 1980) which presumably does not affect brain 5-HT synthesis except perhaps in the area postrema (Koella, 1974).

Tricklebank et al. (1978) also showed that anastomosed rats had decreased responsiveness to mild foot shock. Thus, the mean jump threshold (the lowest voltage at which these rats moved one or more feet from the floor grid) was 32.2 ± 0.9 V. (mean ± S.E.M.) compared with 25.1 ± 1.5 V. in sham-operated rats ($p < 0.005$,

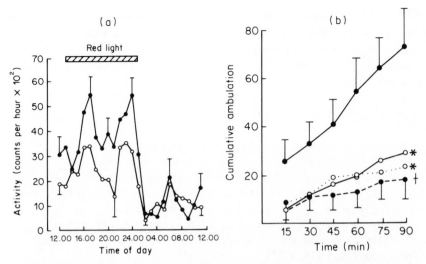

Figure 6. (a) Mean hourly activity score (± S.E.M.) of sham-operated rats (●) and rats with portocaval anastomosis (○) in the home cage over seven successive 24 h periods. Results were analysed by repeated measures analysis of variance. There was a significant effect of anastomosis, $F(1,12) = 5.875, p < 0.05$, and of repeated measure, $F(23,276) = 14.726, p < 0.001$. The difference between the two groups occurred entirely within the red light period $F(1,12) = 6.367, p < 0.05$. N per group = 7 pairs. (b) Mean cumulative ambulation scores in open-field of sham-operated rats given saline (●–●), or L-tryptophan (0.098 mmol kg^{-1} i.p.) (●---●) and rats with portocaval anastomosis given saline (○–○) or L-tryptophan (○···○). For legibility, standard errors are given for sham-operated groups only. They were comparable to those of anastomosed groups. Scorings were over 5 min periods starting at times shown. Terminal scores were compared by analysis of variance followed by Mann-Whitney U test. Significantly different from saline-treated, sham-operated rats: *$p < 0.05$, †$p < 0.005$. N per group = 7. Reproduced by permission of ANKHO International Inc. from Tricklebank et al., 1978

paired comparisons t-test, N = 13 in each group). Tryptophan had a similar effect as in a second experiment, the jump threshold of sham-operated rats was increased from 26.6 ± 1.6 V to 35.1 ± 2.2 V by administration of 0.375 mmol kg^{-1} L-tryptophan x 3 ($p < 0.001$, N = 12 in each group).

It is interesting to note that quite different results were obtained by Salomon et al. (1976) who investigated response to shock not during the active period (red light) as in the above study but during the period when rats normally sleep. Sleep disturbance (Monmaur et al., 1976) was associated with decreased threshold voltage for response to tail-shock.

It might be conjectured that the behavioural effects of anastomosis found by Tricklebank and coworkers simply reflect non-specific hypoactivity. However, hypoactivity did not occur in all test situations, as when pairs of anastomosed rats were brought together during the red light phase after a three-week period of being caged singly, they spent significantly more time engaged in social behaviour than did pairs of sham-operated rats (Table 5). Most of this difference was due to the anastomosed rats sniffing and grooming their partners more frequently than did sham-operated rats.

While there is no evidence that altered tryptophan metabolism is responsible for the increased incidence of social behaviours after anastomosis it is clear that anastomosed rats show a wide range of behavioural abnormalities, at least some of which can be simulated in normal animals by tryptophan administration.

These results suggest that increased tryptophan metabolism could have some responsibility for behavioural changes in liver disease. However, it is only one part of a complicated picture of biochemical and morphological change in the brain. It may well play a part in the altered behaviour but it is hardly likely to be solely responsible for it. This is apparent if one considers that relatively enormous tryptophan intake in normal human subjects only moderately impairs consciousness (Greenwood et al., 1974, 1975).

Other transmitter changes may also be important, in particular the depletion of NA which occurs in acute experimental liver failure (Dodsworth et al., 1974). Various drug experiments are consistent with a role for NA in maintenance of activity (e.g. Dolphin et al., 1976) and it may be that NA depletion together with increased 5-HT synthesis leads to severe impairment of consciousness.

Interest in the possibility that ammonia accumulation had an important role in the genesis of the central symptoms of liver failure (Plum and Hindfelt, 1976) has tended to diminish, partly because relationships between blood ammonia concentrations and the severity of hepatic encephalopathy are not always apparent (Phear et al., 1955; Summerskill et al., 1957). However, James et al. (1979) recently suggested that ammonia facilitates the increase of transmitter precursor amino acid concentrations in the brain, which is thought to be important for the development of central symptoms. They propose that the amino acid change follows an increase of brain glutamine. Such glutamine changes do occur when ammonium acetate is given to normal rats (Hawkins et al., 1973) or in association with the rise of brain ammonia after portocaval anastomosis (Williams et al., 1972). The latter increase of glutamine is greater if the hepatic artery is also ligated (Mans et al., 1979b). James et al. (1979) suggest that the elevated brain glutamine rapidly exchanges with tryptophan, tyrosine, and the other large neutral amino acids in the blood so that their brain:plasma ratios increase. They show that the increased effectiveness of uptake by the brain of these amino acids (Bloxam and Curzon, 1978; James et al., 1978; Mans et al., 1979b) correlates well with brain glutamine concentration. Their hypothesis also provides an explanation of the finding of Norenberg et al. (1974) that rats with a portocaval shunt become comatose when fed on cation resin in the ammonium form.

Table 5. Effect of portocaval anastomosis on social behaviour

Rat observed	Partner	No. of pairs	Behavioural scores		Time in social activity(s)
			Sniffing	Allogrooming	
Sham-operated	Sham operated	14	35 ± 3	2.3 ± 0.4	142 ± 19 (n=7)
Anastomosed	Anastomosed	14	59 ± 4*	7.7 ± 1.2*	290 ± 14* (n=7)

Values are means ± S.E.M. Animals were observed in pairs for 10 min in an observation box 330 × 600 × 300 mm high. They were previously habituated to the box by placing each one in it alone for 10 min on six successive days. Testing commenced on day 8. The frequency of sniffing (the head of one animal orientated towards and close to any part of the body of its partner) and allogrooming (burying of the snout in the fur of its partner) were noted together with the time spent engaged in any form of contact with its partner
Difference from sham-operated: *$p < 0.002$ (Mann-Whitney U test)
Data from Tricklebank et al. (1978)

THERAPEUTIC IMPLICATIONS

The various biochemical disturbances thought to cause brain transmitter changes possibly involved in the development of central symptoms of liver disease may either indicate potential therapeutic procedures or may explain existing therapeutic procedures. For example, the therapeutic effect of intestinal sterilization (Dodsworth et al., 1973) is to some extent explicable in terms of reduced ammonia formation. Also a number of groups have found that central symptoms were diminished on giving amino acids which compete with tryptophan and tyrosine for transport to the brain. Thus, Smith et al. (1978) infused 23% dextrose plus a specially formulated amino acid mixture (F. 080) containing aromatic and branched chain amino acids at low and high concentrations respectively into dogs with experimental hepatic coma. After 1–8 h the animals began to awake and returned to coma if the infusion was stopped. The infusion also caused the elevated CSF concentrations of octopamine, phenylethanolamine and 5-HIAA to return to normal values. Dextrose plus F. 080 also alleviated symptoms in patients with hepatic encephalopathy (Fischer et al., 1976a).

As Mans et al. (1979a) found that tryptophan transport into the brains of rats with acute hepatic failure was relatively little affected by competing amino acids, it is perhaps surprising that these substances should confer much benefit in other species with hepatic coma. Perhaps transport of tyrosine is more susceptible to competition or perhaps species differences are important. It is worth noting that Mans (1979) found that dextrose alone or dextrose plus F. 080 were comparably effective in decreasing brain tryptophan and tyrosine concentrations in rats with chronic portocaval anastomosis.

It should be possible to adjust transmitter metabolism or function more directly in hepatic coma than by altering amino acid availability. It may be that the transient awakening effect of L-Dopa in hepatic coma (Parkes et al., 1970; Fischer et al., 1976b) is due to a relatively direct mechanism in which the drug causes either the repletion of neuronal NA (Dodsworth et al., 1974) or the removal of neuronal octopamine (James and Fischer, 1975).

SUMMARY

Work on patients with liver disease and on laboratory animals with experimental liver failure reveals increased CSF and brain concentrations of the aromatic amino acids which are transmitter precursors (tryptophan and tyrosine). This is not merely a consequence of altered plasma concentrations of these amino acids but probably reflects a number of changes, including disordered brain uptake mechanisms. These may be influenced by the accumulation of ammonia which occurs in severe liver disease. Also (after food intake at least) plasma insulin can be abnormally raised and can result in decreased plasma concentrations of amino acids competing with tryptophan and tyrosine for access to the brain. In the case of tryptophan an additional mechanism can increase its availability to the brain, as plasma UFA tends to be raised, causing reduced binding of tryptophan to plasma albumin so that free tryptophan (the available form) rises.

The increase of brain tryptophan results in increased 5-HT synthesis. However, the rise of brain tyrosine does not lead to corresponding DA or NA changes, instead, octopamine and related 'trace' amines accumulate and can displace neuronal NA so that its concentration in the brain falls. Evidence suggests that these transmitter changes have some responsibility for the symptoms of hepatic encephalopathy. This conclusion is based on the toxic effects of aromatic amino acids in patients or animals with liver failure and on the association of behavioural abnormalities and altered tryptophan metabolism in rats with portocaval anastomosis. These observations have therapeutic implications. Thus treatments which decrease brain tryptophan and tyrosine alleviate hepatic encephalopathy.

REFERENCES

Baldessarini, R. J., and Fischer, J. F. (1973) Serotonin metabolism in rat brain after surgical diversion of the portal venous circulation. *Nature (New Biol.)*, **245**, 25–27.

Beaubernard, C., Salomon, F., Grange, D., Thangapregassam, M. J., and Bismuth, J. (1977) Experimental hepatic encephalopathy. Changes of the level of wakefulness in the rat with portocaval anastomosis. *Biomedicine*, **27**, 169–171.

Bloxam, D. L., and Curzon, G. (1978) A study of proposed determinants of brain tryptophan concentration in rats after portocaval anastomosis or sham operation. *J. Neurochem.*, **31**, 1255–1263.

Bloxam, D. L., Tricklebank, M. D., Patel, A. J., and Curzon, G. (1980) Effects of albumin, amino acids, and clofibrate on the uptake of tryptophan by the rat brain. *J. Neurochem.*, **34**, 43–49.

Buxton, G. H., Stewart, D. A., Murray-Lyon, I. M., Curzon, G., and Williams, R. (1974) Plasma amino acids in acute hepatic failure and their relationship to brain tryptophan. *Clin. Sci. Mol. Med.*, **46**, 555–562.

Condon, R. E. (1971) Effect of dietary protein on symptoms and survival in dogs with an Eck fistula. *Am. J. Surg.*, **121**, 107–114.

Cremer, J. E., Teal, H. M., Heath, D. F., and Cavanagh, J. B. (1977) The influence of portocaval anastomosis on the metabolism of labelled octanoate, butyrate, and leucine in rat brain. *J. Neurochem.*, **28**, 215–222.

Cummings, M. G., James, J. H., Soeters, P. B., Keane, J. M., Foster, J., and Fischer, J. E. (1976a) Regional brain study of indoleamine metabolism in the rat in acute hepatic failure. *J. Neurochem.*, **27**, 741–746.

Cummings, M. G., Soeters, P. B. James, J. H., Keane, J. M., and Fischer, J. E. (1976b) Regional brain indoleamine metabolism following chronic porto-caval anastomosis in the rat. *J. Neurochem.*, **27**, 501–509.

Curzon, G. (1979) Relationships between plasma, CSF and brain tryptophan. *J. Neural Trans.*, **Suppl. 15**, 81–92.

Curzon, G., and Knott, P. J. (1974) Effects on plasma and brain tryptophan in the rat of drugs and hormones that influence the concentration of unesterified fatty acids in the plasma. *Br. J. Pharmac.*, **37**, 689–697.

Curzon, G., Friedel, J., and Knott, P. J. (1973a) The effects of fatty acids on the binding of tryptophan to plasma proteins. *Nature,* 242, 198–200.

Curzon, G., Kantamaneni, B. D., Winch, J., Rojas-Bueno, A., Murray-Lyon, I. M., and Williams, R. (1973b) Plasma and brain tryptophan changes in experimental acute hepatic failure. *J. Neurochem.,* 21, 137–145.

Curzon, G., Friedel, J., Kantamaneni, B. D., Greenwood, M. H., and Lader, M. H. (1974) Unesterified fatty acids and the binding of tryptophan in human plasma. *Clin. Sci. Mol. Med.,* 47., 415–424.

Curzon, G., Kantamaneni, B. D., Fernando, J. C., Woods, M. S., and Cavanagh, J. B. (1975) Effects of chronic portocaval anastomosis on brain tryptophan, tyrosine and 5-hydroxytryptamine, *J. Neurochem.,* 24, 1065–1070.

Curzon, G., Kantamaneni, B. D., Bartlett, J. R., and Bridges, P. K. (1976) Transmitter precursors and metabolites in human ventricular cerebrospinal fluid. *J. Neurochem.,* 26, 613–615.

Daniel, P. M. Love, E. R., Moorhouse, S. R., and Pratt, O. E. (1979) Effect of insulin upon levels of amino acids in the blood and upon the influx of tryptophan into the brain. *J. Physiol.,* 289, 87–88P.

Delafosse, B., Bouletreau, P., and Motin, J. (1977) Variation des acides aminés plasmatiques au cours des hepatites graves avec encéphalopathie. *Nouv. Presse Med.,* 6, 1207–1211.

Dodsworth, J. M. Cummings, M. G., James, J. H., and Fischer, J. E. (1973) The effects of intestinal sterilization on brain amines. *Gastroenterology,* 64, 881.

Dodsworth, J. M., James, J. H., Cummings, M. G., and Fischer, J. E. (1974) Depletion of brain norepinephrine in acute hepatic coma. *Surgery,* 75, 811–820.

Dolphin, A., Jenner, P., and Marsden, C. D. (1976) Noradrenaline synthesis from L-Dopa in rodents and its relationship to motor activity. *Pharmac. Biochem. Behav.,* 5, 431–439.

Eccleston, D., Ashcroft, G. W., and Crawford, T. B. B. (1965) 5-Hydroxyindole metabolism in rat brain. A study of intermediate metabolism using the technique of tryptophan loading. II Applications and drug studies. *J. Neurochem.* 12, 493–503.

Elithorn, A., Lunzer, M., and Weinman, J. (1975) Cognitive effects associated with chronic hepatic encephalopathy and their response to levodopa. *J, Neurol. Neurosug. Psychiat.,* 38, 794–798.

Fernstrom, J. D., Arnold, M. A., Wurtman, R. J., Hammarstrom-Wiklund, B., Munro, H. N., and Davidson, C. S. (1978) Diurnal variations in plasma insulin concentrations in normal and cirrhotic subjects: effect of dietary protein. *J. Neural Trans.,* Suppl. 14, 133–142.

Fischer, J. E. (1975) On the occurrence of false neurochemical transmitters, in Williams, R., and Murray-Lyon, I. M., (eds.) *Artificial Liver Support* Pitman Medical, London, pp. 31–50.

Fischer, J. E., and Baldessarini, T. (1971) False neurotransmitters and hepatic failure. *Lancet,* ii, 75–80.

Fischer, J. E. Rosen, H. M. Ebeid, A. M.,James, J. H., Keane, J. M., and Soeters, P. B. (1976a) The effect of normalization of plasma amino acids on hepatic encephalopathy in man. *Surgery,* 80, 77–91.

Fischer, J. E., Funovics, J. M. Falcao, H. A., and Wesdorp, R. I. C. (1976b) L-Dopa in hepatic coma. *Ann. Surg.,* 183, 386–391.

Friedman, P. A., Kappelman, A. H., and Kaufman, S. (1972) Partial purification and characterization of tryptophan hydroxylase from rabbit hindbrain. *J. Biol. Chem.,* 247, 4165–4173.

Gal, E. M., Young, R. B., and Sherman, A. D. (1978) Tryptophan loading: conse-quent effects on the synthesis of kynurenine and 5-hydroxyindoles in rat brain. *J. Neurochem.*, **31**, 237–244.

Gentil, V., Lader, M. H., Kantamaneni, B. D., and Curzon, G. (1977) Effects of adrenaline injection on human plasma tryptophan and non-esterified fatty acids. *Clin. Sci. Mol. Med.*, **53**, 227–232.

Gibson, C. J., and Wurtman, R. J. (1978) Physiological control of brain norepine-phrine synthesis by brain tyrosine concentration. *Life Sci.*, **22**, 1399–1406.

Greenwood, M. H., Friedel, J., Bond, A. J., Curzon, G., and Lader, M. H. (1974) The acute effects of intravenous infusion of L-tryptophan in normal subjects. *Clin. Pharmac. Therap.*, **16**, 455–464.

Greenwood, M. H., Lader, M. H., Kantamaneni, B. D., and Curzon, G. (1975) The acute effects of oral (−) tryptophan in human subjects. *Br. J. Clin. Pharmac.*, **2**, 165–172.

Harmar, A. J., and Horn, A. S. (1976) Octopamine in mammalian brain: rapid post-mortem increase and effects of drugs. *J. Neurochem.*, **26**, 987–993.

Hawkins, R. A., Miller, A L., Nielsen, R. C., and Veech, R. L. (1973) The acute action of ammonia on rat brain metabolism *in vivo. Biochem. J.*, **134**, 1001–1008.

Hirayama, L. (1971) Tryptophan metabolism in liver disease. *Clin Chim. Acta,* **32**, 191–197.

Homlin, T., and Siesjo, B. K. (1974) The effect of porto-caval anastomosis upon the energy state and upon acid–base parameters of the rat brain. *J. Neurochem.*, **22**, 403–412.

Iber, F. L., Rosen, H., Stanley, M., Tevenson, M. O., and Chalmers, T. C. (1957) The plasma amino acids in patients with liver failure. *J. Lab. Clin. Med.*, **50**, 417–425.

James, J. H., and Fischer, J. E. (1975) Release of octopamine and α-methylocto-pamine by L-Dopa. *J. Neurochem.*, **24**, 1099–1101.

James, J. H., Hodgman, J. M. Funovics, J. M., and Fischer, J. E. (1976) Alterations in brain octopamine and brain tyrosine following portocaval anastomosis in rats. *J. Neurochem.*, **27**, 223–227.

James, J. H., Escourrou, J., and Fischer, J. E. (1978) Blood-brain neutral amino acid transport activity is increased after portocaval anastomosis. *Science,* **200**, 1395–1397.

James, J. H., Ziparo, V., Jeppson, B. and Fischer, J. E. (1979) Hyperammonaemia, plasma amino acid imbalance and blood–brain amino acid transport: a unified theory of portal-systemic encephalopathy. *Lancet*, **ii**, 772–775.

Jellinger, K., and Riederer, P. (1977) Brain monoamines in metabolic (endotoxic) coma. A preliminary biochemical study in human post-mortem material. *J. Neural Trans.*, **41**, 275–286.

Jellinger, K. Riederer, P., Kleinberger, G., Wuketich, S., and Kothbauer, P. (1978) Brain monoamines in human hepatic encephalopathy. *Acta Neuropathol. (Berl),* **43**, 63–68.

Jouvet, M. (1968) Insomnia and decrease of cerebral 5-hydroxytryptamine after destruction of the raphe system in the cat. *Adv. Pharmac.*, **6B**, 265–282.

Knell, A. J., Davidson, A. R., Williams, R., Kantamaneni, B. D., and Curzon, G. (1974) Dopamine and serotonin metabolism in hepatic encephalopathy. *Br. Med. J.* i. 549–551.

Koella, W. P. (1974) Serotonin–a hypnogenic transmitter and anti-waking agent. *Adv. Biochem. Psychopharmac.*, **11**, 181–186.

Knott, P. J., and Curzon, G. (1972) Free tryptophan in plasma and brain trypto-phan metabolism. *Nature,* **239**, 452–453.

Knott, P. J., and Curzon, G. (1975) Tryptophan and tyrosine disposition and brain tryptophan metabolism in acute carbon tetrachloride poisoning. *Biochem. Pharmac.,* **24**, 963–966.

Knott, P. J., Hutson, P. H., and Curzon, G. (1977) Fatty acid and tryptophan changes on disturbing groups of rats and caging them singly. *Pharmac. Biochem. Behav.,* **7**, 245–252.

Laursen, H., Klysner, R., and Geisler, A, (1977) Adenylate cyclase activity in corpus striatum of rats with porto-caval anastomoses. *Acta Physiol. Scand.,* **100**, 282–287.

Mans, A. M. (1979) *Neurotransmitter alterations in hepatic failure: influence of precursor distribution and blood–brain barrier transport.* Ph. D. Thesis, Capetown.

Mans, A. M., Biebuyck, J. F., Saunders, S. J., Kirsch, R. E., and Hawkins, R. A. (1979a) Tryptophan transport across the blood–brain barrier during acute hepatic failure. *J. Neurochem.,* **33**, 409–418.

Mans, A. M., Saunders, S. J., Kirsch, R. E., and Biebuyck, J. F. (1976b) Correlations of plasma and brain amino acids and putative neurotransmitter alterations during acute hepatic coma in the rat. *J. Neurochem.,* **32**, 285–292.

McMenamy, R. H. (1965) Binding of indole analogues to human serum albumin. Effects of fatty acids. *J. Biol. Chem.,* **24**, 4235–4243.

Molinoff, P. B., and Buck, S. H. (1976) Octopamine: normal occurence in neuronal tissues of rats and other species, in Usdin, E., and Sandler, M. (eds.) *Trace Amines and the Brain* Dekker, New York and Basel, pp. 131–160.

Monmaur, P. Beaubernard, C., Salomon, F., Grange, D., Thangapregassam, M. J., and Bismuth, H. (1976) Encephalopathie hepatique experimentale. Modifications de la duree des differents etats de sommeil diurne chez le rat avec anastomose porto-cave. *Biol. Gastroenterol. (Paris),* **9**, 99–103.

Munro, H. N., Fernstrom, J. D., and Wurtman, R. J. (1975) Insulin, plasma amino acid imbalance and hepatic coma. *Lancet,* **i**, 722–724.

Norenberg, M. D., Lapham, L. W., Nichols, F. A., and May, A. G. (1974) An experimental model for the study of hepatic encephalopathy. *Arch. Neurol.,* **31**, 106–109.

Ogihara, K., Mozai, T., and Hirai, S. (1966) Tryptophan as cause of hepatic coma. *New Engl. J. Med.,* **275**, 1255–1256.

Ono, J. Hutson, D. G., Dombro, R. S., Levi, J. U., Livingstone, A., and Zeppa, R. (1978) Tryptophan and hepatic coma. *Gastroenterology,* **74**, 196–200.

Pardridge, W. M., and Oldendorf, W. H. (1975) Kinetic analysis of blood–brain barrier transport of amino acids. *Biochim. Biophys. Acta,* **401**, 128–136.

Parkes, J. D., Sharpstone, P., and Williams, R. (1970) Levodopa in hepatic coma. *Lancet,* **ii**, 1341–1343.

Parrilla, R., Goodman, M. N., and Toews, C. J. (1974) Effect of glucagon: insulin ratio on hepatic metabolism. *Diabetes,* **23**, 725–731.

Phear, E. A., Sherlock, S., and Summerskill, W. H. J. (1955) Blood-ammonium levels in liver disease and 'hepatic coma' *Lancet,* **i**, 836–840.

Plum, F., and Hindfelt, B. (1976) The neurological complications of liver disease. *Handbook of Clinical Neurology,* **27**, 349–377.

Record, C. D., Buxton, B., Chase, R. A., Curzon, G., Murray-Lyon, I. M., and Williams, R. (1976) Plasma and brain amino acids in fulminant hepatic failure and their relationship to hepatic encephalopathy. *Eur. J. Clin. Invest.,* **6**, 387–394.

Robison, G. A., Butcher, R. W., and Sutherland, K. W. (1971) *Cyclic AMP,* Academic Press, New York, and London.

Rossi-Fanelli, F., Cangiano, C., Attili, A., Angelico, M., Cascino, A., Cappocaccia, L.,

Strom, R., and Crifo, C. (1976) Octopamine plasma levels and hepatic encephalopathy: a reappraisal of the problem. *Clin. Chim. Acta.,* **67**, 255–261.

Salomon, F., Beaubernard, C., Thangapregassam, M. J., Grange, D., and Bismuth, H. (1976) Encephalopathie hepatique experimentale. II. Etude de la reaction à la douleur chez le rat avec anastomose porto-cave. *Biol. Gastroenterol. (Paris),* **9**, 105–108.

Sherlock, S. (1968) *Diseases of the Liver and Biliary System,* Blackwell, Oxford, p. 84.

Smith, J. E. Lane, J D., Shea, P. A., and McBride, W. J. (1977) Neurochemical changes following the administration of precursors of biogenic amines. *Life Sci.* **21**, 301–306.

Smith, A. R., Rossi-Fanelli, P., Ziparo, V., James, J. H., Perelle, B. A., and Fischer, J. E. (1978) Alterations in plasma and CSF amino acids, amines and metabolites in hepatic coma. *Ann. Surg.,* **187**, 343–350.

Sourkes, T. L. (1978) Tryptophan in hepatic coma. *J. Neural Trans.,* **Suppl. 14**, 79–86.

Summerskill, W. H. J., Wolfe, S. J. and Davidson, C. S. (1957) The metabolism of ammonia and α-keto acids in liver disease and hepatic coma. *J. Clin. Invest.,* **36**, 361–372.

Sved, A. F., Fernstrom, J. D., and Wurtman, R. J. (1979) Tyrosine administration reduces blood pressure and enhances brain norepinephrine release in spontaneously hypertensive rats. *Proc. Nat. Acad. Sci.* USA, **76**, 3511–3514.

Taggart, P., and Carruthers, M. (1971) Endogenous hyperlipidaemia induced by emotional stress of racing driving. *Lancet*, **i**, 363–366.

Taylor, M. (1976) Effects of L-tryptophan and L-methionine on activity in the rat. *Br. J. Pharmac.,* **58**, 117–119.

Tricklebank, M. D., Drewitt, P. N., and Curzon, G. (1980) The effect of L-tryptophan on motor activity and its prevention by an extracerebral decarboxylase inhibitor and by 5-HT receptor blockers. *Psychopharmac.* (in press).

Tricklebank, M. D., Smart, J. L., Bloxam, D. L., and Curzon, G. (1978) Effects of chronic experimental liver dysfunction and L-tryptophan on behaviour in the rat. *Pharmac. Biochem. Behav.,* **9**, 181–189.

Unger, R. H. (1971) Glucagon physiology and pathophysiology. *New Engl. J. Med.,* **285**, 443–449.

Williams, A. H., Kyu, M. H., Fenton, J. C. B., and Cavanagh, J. B. (1972) The glutamate and glutamine content of rat brain after portocaval anastomosis. *J. Neurochem.,* **19**, 1073–1077.

Wurtman, R. J., and Fernstrom, J. D. (1976) Control of brain neurotransmitter synthesis by precursor availability and nutritional state. *Biochem. Pharmac.,* **25**, 1691–1696.

Yuwiler, A., Oldendorf, W. H. Geller, E., and Braun, L. (1977) Effect of albumin binding and amino acid competition on tryptophan uptake into brain. *J. Neurochem.,* **28**, 1015–1023.

The Biochemistry of Psychiatric Disturbances
Edited by G. Curzon
© 1980 John Wiley & Sons Ltd.

CHAPTER 7

Biochemistry of Alzheimer's Disease

DAVID M. BOWEN AND A. N. DAVISON

INTRODUCTION

There are many causes of the clinical state dementia. Excluding those patients with symptoms associated with tumours, infections, or vascular disease there remains a large group (Corsellis, 1962, Katzman, 1976) whose brains are atrophied with an excess of senile degenerative changes (senile plaques, neurofibrillary, and granulovacuolar degeneration) in the neocortex and hippocampus. Altered presynaptic axon terminals, presynaptic neurites associated with senile plaques and a decrease in the density of dendritic spines have also been described (for references see Bowen et al., 1976a, 1977a). When this condition occurs before the age of 65 years it is known as presenile dementia or Alzheimer's disease; after this age it has been called senile dementia or senile dementia of Alzheimer's type. Since there is no good reason on neurological grounds (Corsellis, 1976) to maintain this distinction for all but the rare familial cases (Scheibel and Tomiyasu, 1978) the term Alzheimer's disease is used in this chapter irrespective of the patient's age. The disease is generally accepted to be the commonest organic cause of intellectual deterioration: more psychiatric hospital patients die with it than with schizophrenia (Figure 1). Although Alzheimer's disease is prevalent, there is still considerable uncertainty about its pathogenesis and little is known about aetiology.

There have been three main approaches to the study of the chemical pathology of organic dementia: examination of lesioned brain material and either subcellular fractionation or direct analysis of brain material.

The examination of the well-defined histological lesions by histochemistry and biochemical separation techniques has shown:

(1)   The 'core' of senile plaques may contain IgG (Ishii and Haga, 1976), suggesting that immunological factors are involved in pathogenesis.

(2)   An unexplained finding of high silicon concentration in the 'cores' and 'rims' of senile plaques (Nikaido et al., 1972).

(3)   A localized increase in the activity of oxidative enzymes in senile plaques (Ishii, 1969; Friede, 1965; Friede and Magee, 1962) which is probably due to the projection of processes from astrocytes.

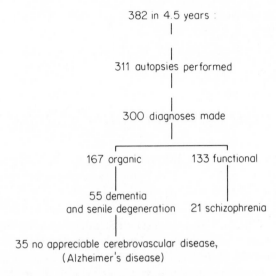

Figure 1. Number of deaths due to Alzheimer's disease and schizophrenia in a psychiatric hospital (data from Corsellis, 1962)

(4)   Neurons containing neurofibrillary tangles may contain an abnormal protein of neurofilamentous origin (Shelanski, 1978).

(5)   Nerve cells in Alzheimer's disease contain no more lipofuscin ageing pigment than cells of a control group (Mann and Sinclair, 1978), suggesting that the disease is not an exacerbation of normal ageing.

(6)   Granulovacuoles show a positive reaction for acid phosphatase and other acid hydrolases (Krigman et al., 1965), suggesting changes in lysosomes.

Subcellular fractionation of post-mortem brain tissue was pioneered by Stahl et al. (1971). As judged by protein content and 'marker' enzyme activity measurements, subcellular fractionation of post-mortem brain tissue from patients dying suddenly and fresh animal brain, yield similar results. In contrast, electron microscopy and neurotransmitter uptake measurements on subcellular fractions indicate that the yield of synaptosomes with well-preserved structure and metabolic activity is low from post-mortem specimens (Bowen et al., 1977a). Protein analysis of subcellular fractions from the neocortex of cases of Alzheimer's disease (Bowen et al., 1973) suggest that as much as half of the subcellular organelles are recovered in the nuclear pellet. Further studies (Smith, 1976) suggest that it contains organelles that are normally isolated in the crude mitochondrial fraction. This phenomenon can, in part, be mimicked by varying the physicochemical properties of tissue homogenates (Smith, 1976; White, 1978).

The above sources of error are excluded if homogenates of human brain in buffered sucrose are centrifuged at 15,000 X g and the resulting pellet subjected to discontinuous sucrose density gradient centrifugation. Using this method the protein content of fractions isolated from brains of subjects with Alzheimer's disease has been determined (White *et al.*, 1978). Control human brains were also examined. Furthermore, as the morphological hallmarks of Alzheimer's disease are not often found in the caudate nucleus, fractions isolated from this region were used as internal controls. Although one fraction (the interphase between 0.32 M and 0.8 M sucrose solution) may be abnormal in the neocortex of Alzheimer brains the results did not reveal extensive differences between Alzheimer and control tissue. Electron microscopic examination of the fraction at the interphase between 0.8 M and 1.2 M sucrose solutions from both Alzheimer and control samples showed synaptosomes (some intact with postsynaptic adhesions but others in a relatively poor state of preservation) and 'dense bodies' of indeterminate origin. The state of preservation of synaptosomes from control biopsy samples, however, is good (White, 1978). Therefore biopsy samples from Alzheimer cases should be investigated. Studies of this type have already been of value in elucidating the pathogenesis of extraneural diseases (Peters, 1977).

Biochemical analyses of unfractionated brain tissue are of proved value in the elucidation of neurotransmitter abnormalities in Parkinson's disease and Huntington's chorea. Similar studies on brain samples of Alzheimer's disease provide information about the extent and selectivity of cellular changes such as neuronal loss and also whether the disease is an accelerated form of normal ageing. These studies are described below.

GLIAL CELLS

Cathepsin A activity, a potential marker of microglia or brain macrophages (Bowen and Davison, 1974) is high in senile brain (Bowen *et al.*, 1977b), which conforms with the established view that cells of this type occur in Alzheimer brain.

It is often assumed that astrocytes greatly increase in number in areas of brain undergoing degenerative change, although work on the striatum of subjects with Huntington's chorea suggests that this is not so (Lange *et al.*, 1976). Preliminary attempts to assess the relative number of 'macroglia' (astrocytes and oligodendrocytes) in the temporal lobe of Alzheimer brain, using β-glucuronidase and carbonic anhydrase activities as markers suggest that glial cells survive better than neurons in the Alzheimer brain (Bowen *et al.*, 1977b). Further work indicates that neuronal degeneration precedes the change in the glial marker enzymes (Bowen *et al.*, 1979). Thus neurons appear to be selectively affected in Alzheimer's disease.

NEURONAL LOSS

The narrowing of the cortical ribbon and loss in brain weight in Alzheimer's disease and possibly also in normal ageing has been ascribed to neuronal fallout. As cortical cell counts (Terry *et al.*, 1977; Tomlinson and Henderson, 1976) yield no measure of total cell numbers, current morphological methods are of limited value in testing such a hypothesis. Therefore, we have used biochemical methods to assess cellular and subcellular changes in brain. The analyses were carried out on aliquots of whole temporal lobe and the results were expressed per lobe, thus reducing errors due to oedema, water loss, or differences in tissue sampling. The temporal lobe was studied because it is particularly affected in Alzheimer's disease.

The content of DNA, ganglioside, myelin protein, ratio of DNA to RNA, and activities of β-galactosidase and adenosine 2,3-cyclic nucleotide 3-phosphohydrolase (phosphohydrolase) were measured as potential indices of nerve cell number. None of these markers altered significantly with age in temporal lobe from histologically normal brains of non-demented subjects aged 50 to 100 years, living normal lives appropriate to their age. Due to either secondary glial reactions (Bowen *et al.*, 1977b), post-mortem artefact (Smith and Bowen, 1976) or terminal changes (Bowen *et al.*, 1977b), only ganglioside content (marker of nerve cell membranes) and phosphohydrolase activity (marker of myelinated axons) appeared to be reasonably reliable as quantitative markers in the temporal lobe. In Alzheimer's disease both constituents are significantly (p usually < 0.01) reduced to 57–70% of the control values when matched for post-mortem handling, terminal status, and age (Bowen *et al.*, 1977b, 1979). Comparison of preliminary data for lobes from patients who had died in similar circumstances suggests that the reduced contents of DNA (to 80% of control, $p < 0.02$) and RNA (to 46% of control, $p < 0.01$) in Alzheimer's disease (Bowen *et al.*, 1977b) are not epiphenomena but reflect both cell shrinkage and loss of cell body material (Nissl substance). The reduced ganglioside content agrees with data expressed per unit mass (Suzuki *et al.*, 1965; Cherayil, 1969), while the reduced RNA content is consistent with histochemical data (Mann and Sinclair, 1978).

It can be concluded that the neocortical neurons of the temporal lobe, representing much of the massive neocortical development in man, normally survive into old age but in Alzheimer's disease there is significant shrinkage and probably loss of these neurons. This suggests that Alzheimer's disease is a primary degenerative nerve cell disorder and not the result of accelerated ageing. However, some neurons are unaffected as Uemura and Hartmann (1978) were able to isolate normal neocortical neuronal perikarya from Alzheimer brain. Similarly, precise morphological measurements (Ball, 1977, 1978) indicate that not all hippocampal neurons are affected.

SELECTIVE VULNERABILITY

Senile plaques are often associated with capillaries (Miyakawa *et al.*, 1974) which suggests that neurons which are selectively affected may be vulnerable because of proximity to an extra-neural toxic factor. Aluminium, lead, or an antibody (Crapper *et al.*, 1976; Niklowitz, 1975; Ishii and Haga, 1976) have been implicated. Oxygen deprivation, already implicated in the rarer dementia of Huntington's chorea (Bowen *et al.*, 1976b) may also be implicated in the hippocampal damage as this is similar in hypoxic and Alzheimer brain (Ball, 1978).

TERMINAL DAMAGE IN DEMENTIA

Subcellular fractionation data suggests that abnormally high amounts of lysosomal cathepsin and β-galactosidase activity is released into the cytoplasm in brains of demented patients (Bowen et al., 1973). Although there was little loss of soluble brain protein (except from the pre-frontal cortex in severely ischemic patients) this led us to study whether there was a selective loss of protein susceptible to catheptic action. By examining buffered hypotonic extracts of grey matter by porosity gradient polyacrylamide gels (Grossgeld and Shooter, 1971) we found that a soluble acidic protein (which we termed neuronin S-6) was frequently absent from all regions of the brain in Alzheimer's disease (Bowen et al., 1973; Smith and Bowen, 1976), even from those such as the thalamus which exhibited little pathological change.

Neuronin-type protein was estimated by direct densitometry using procian brilliant blue as stain. Neuronin S-6 separated as a sharp band below serum albumin and above 14:3:3 (M.W. 52,000), and constituted about 1% of water-soluble grey matter protein. It could be distinguished from numerous other proteins. Thus, antisera to human GFA protein or rat antigen-α (14:3:2) did not cross-react and it differed in mobility from S-100 and human serum albumin on gradient porosity gels. In sodium dodecyl sulphate (SDS) acrylamide gels it could be differentiated from antigen-α (rat brain), 14:3:2 (bovine brain), tubulin (rat brain) and albumin. The molecular weight was about 47,000 (SDS polyacrylamide), close to that of the actin-like acidic protein neurin (M.W. 43,000 isolated by Puszkin et al., 1972). However, unlike this protein, neuronin S-6 did not contain 3-methylhistidine or activate Mg^{2+}-dependent myosin ATPase (Smith, 1976). Peptide maps (Bray and Brownlee, 1973) showed a unique pattern in comparison to other acidic brain proteins (tubulin, actin, neurofilament, and 14:3:2 protein) a characteristic negatively charged peptide being present (Smith et al., 1974; Smith, 1976).

Neuronin S-6 is remarkably stable to post-mortem storage, e.g. 18 h at $37\,^{\circ}C$ (Bowen et al., 1976a) but was depleted in patients with bronchopneumonia (most Alzheimer cases) and non-demented subjects dying with 'oxygen deprivation', especially in the depths of the cerebral cortical sulci where the oxygen supply may be especially restricted. As it is insoluble at pH = 5 failure to detect it may be due to the fall in intracellular pH resulting from hypoxia. Glutamate decarboxylase (GAD) also is susceptible to hypoxia, which appears to explain the lower activity found in controls dying of bronchopneumonia (Table 1). This was shown by subjecting baboons to cortical ischemia by experimental middle cerebral artery occlusion. In areas of dense ischemia there was a significant decrease in neuronin S-6 concentration, GABA uptake, and GAD activity, a slight decrease in choline uptake (Goodhardt et al., 1977; Strong et al., 1977), but no change in other specific proteins. It may be concluded that depletions of neuronin S-6 and GAD are indices of terminal anoxia and are not directly related to the pathogenesis of brain atrophy. In agreement with this, preliminary results indicate that GAD activity is normal in biopsy samples from patients with Alzheimer's and related diseases (Bowen and Davison, 1978).

Table 1. CAT and GAD activities and senile degeneration in Alzheimer's disease

Diagnosis	CAT activity (nmol g tissue^{-1} min^{-1})	GAD activity (μmol g tissue^{-1} h^{-1})	Senile plaques (rel. score*)	Neurofibrillary degeneration (rel. score*)	Neuronal loss (rel. score*)
Alzheimer's disease†:					
Patient 1	3.87	1.04	2	0	2
Patient 2	3.57	1.74	2	1	1
Patient 3	2.78	1.92	2	1	1
Patient 4	2.22	1.11	3	3	2
Patient 5	2.05	0.98	2–3	1	n.d.
Patient 6	2.03	1.01	3	3	2
Mean	2.75 ± 0.80 (6)‡	1.30 ± 0.42 (6)‡	n.d.	n.d.	n.d.
Controls					
Bronchopneumonia deaths (7)	5.40 ± 1.23 (7)	3.11 ± 0.82 (8)§	—	—	—
Sudden deaths (12)	4.68 ± 1.10 (12)	4.88 ± 2.06 (17)	—	—	—

Modified from Bowen *et al.* (1976a)
Number of cases in parentheses ± S.D.; – none or trace; n.d. not determined
*Scale 0–3 (none to severe). † Died of bronchopneumonia. ‡Significantly different (p at least < 0.01) from both control groups. §Significantly different (p < 0.05) from value for controls with sudden deaths

VULNERABILITY OF CHOLINERGIC NEURONS

Choline acetyl transferase (CAT) activity appears to be relatively unaffected by terminal bronchopneumonia and severe 'cerebral' hypoxia. Thus, while Alzheimer's disease patients who had died of bronchopneumonia (Table 1), show no correspondence between GAD activities and senile degeneration (senile plaque formation and neurofibrillary degeneration or tangle formation) there is a semiquantitative relationship between the two histological variables and CAT activity. The same relationship may also occur in patients who died suddenly: Patient A (plaques 1–2, tangles 0, CAT 0.21 unit) and Patient B (plaques 3, tangles 1, CAT 0.14 unit). As CAT activity was not age-dependent, patients were matched with controls of similar terminal status (Table 1). The activity appeared to be significantly reduced in Alzheimer's disease (Bowen et al., 1976a) which is of considerable interest as Perry et al. (1978b) find a significant correlation between mental test score and CAT activity of depressed and Alzheimer patients (Figure 2).

Of 35 biochemical constituents measured in the whole temporal lobe, 19 are significantly reduced in Alzheimer's disease. The whole lobe weight is least affected and apart from neuronin S-6 CAT activity is the most depleted component (reduced to at least 35% of control $p < 0.001$, Table 2). Furthermore, CAT activity is also low in biopsy samples from patients with Alzheimer's disease (Figure 3). This appears to precede widespread structural damage to neurons as gangliosides, which are probably distributed over the entire neuronal surface (Ledeen, 1978), are not reduced in biopsy material (Blackwood and Cumings, 1959). As we find that CAT activity is not age-dependent in controls expressed either per temporal lobe or per unit mass (Bowen et al., 1979) the change in cortical CAT activity does not appear to be the result of accelerated ageing. However, Perry et al. (1977b) report that in controls CAT activity does decline with advancing age (particularly in hippocampus) and conclude that there is a 'cholinergic connection between normal ageing and senile dementia'.

The finding of reduced post-mortem CAT activity has been confirmed in subsequent studies in our laboratory and by independent investigations (Table 3). Also, Perry et al. (1978b) have shown the relationship between intensity of senile degeneration and decrease of CAT activity. Acetylcholinesterase activity is also reduced (Davies and Maloney, 1976; Bowen et al., 1977b; Perry et al., 1978a), which is further evidence for disturbed acetylcholine metabolism in Alzheimer's disease.

CHANGES IN OTHER CORTICAL TRANSMITTER SYSTEMS

Muscarinic cholinoreceptive cells, measured using atropine (White et al., 1977; Bowen et al., 1979), scopolamine (Perry et al., 1977a) or quinuclidinyl benzilate (Davies and Verth, 1978; Bowen et al., 1979) appear normal in Alzheimer's disease, as does high affinity binding of dihydroaloprenolol (measured as an index of β-adrenergic receptors; Bowen et al., 1979). Histochemical results (Berger et al., 1976) and the finding of reduced amounts of NA in Alzheimer's disease brains

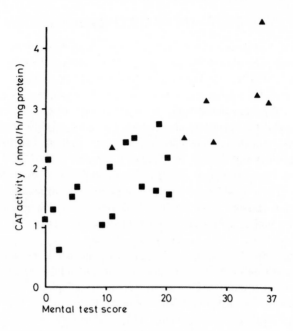

Figure 2.   Relation between cortical CAT activity and mental test score (r = 0.81, $p < 0.001$) for Alzheimer's disease (■) and depressed patients (▲) combined. Modified from Perry *et al.*, 1978b

Table 2. Selected changes in whole temporal lobe

Potential indices	Significant ($p < 0.01$) changes in Alzheimer's disease (content % control)
Cholinergic neurons (CAT)	35
Number of nerve cells (ganglioside NANA; phosphohydrolase)	60–70
Serotoninergic system (5-HIAA; 5-HIAA/5-HT; high affinity LSD binding)	
Atrophy (lobe weight; total protein)	77–81

Modified from Bowen *et al.* (1979)
Results for 17 subjects with Alzheimer's disease and 16 control subjects
Abbreviations: 5-HIAA, 5-hydroxyindoleacetic acid; 5-HT, serotonin; LSD, lysergic acid diethylamide

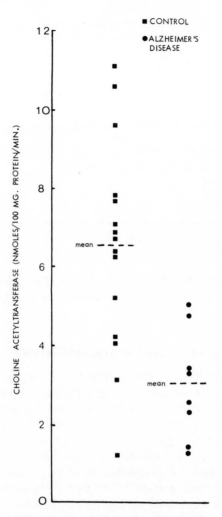

Figure 3.   CAT activity in grey matter
from cortical biopsies. Mean values
differ significantly ($p < 0.01$) for the
two groups. Modified from Bowen *et
al.*, 1979

(Adolfson *et al.*, 1978) suggest that NAergic cells are affected. Reisine *et al.* (1978)
report that GABA receptor binding (measured using GABA) is depleted while Bowen
et al. (1979) find that the receptor binding (measured using muscimol) is age-
dependent in elderly controls but not in age-matched Alzheimer cases. Deterioration of 5-HT pathways is also indicated, for the high affinity binding of LSD
(Bowen *et al.*, 1979) and the 5-HT metabolite 5-HIAA are decreased (Table 3).

Table 3.   Neocortical CAT activities measured ante- and post-mortem

Tissue	CAT activity Control (nmol min^{-1} 100 mg protein^{-1})	Alzheimer's disease (% control†)
Biopsy: (Figure 3)	6.5	46
Autopsy:		
Bowen et al. (1976a)*	7.2	51
Davies and Maloney (1976)*	15.2	35
Perry et al. (1977a)	3.9	31
Reisine et al. (1978)	8.3	40
White et al. (1977)	5.4	50

*Calculated from data expressed per g fresh weight
†p at least < 0.05, usually < 0.01

Thus, there are indications of changes in several neurotransmitter system, as has now been found in other degenerative disorders (e.g. Huntington's chorea and Parkinson's disease).

PEPTIDE NEUROMODULATORS

Few of the 15 or so neuropeptide candidates for a modulator or transmitter role have been investigated in diseased brain and only fragmentary data is available. For example, immunoreactivity to vasoactive intestinal peptide, which is present at particularly high concentrations in cortex, is reduced in CSF of patients with cerebral atrophy (Fahrenkrug et al., 1977). Vasopressin acts on some brain regions, including the hippocampus, facilitating the consolidation of memory (Wimersma-Greidanus and de Wied, 1977) and may be of use in human memory disorders (Legros et al., 1978; Oliveros et al., 1978) Opiate receptor binding (measured using naloxone) and angiotensin converting enzyme activity are not significantly abnormal in temporal lobe from patients with Alzheimer's disease. However, the converting enzyme is age-dependent in the Alzheimer samples, but not in age-matched controls (Bowen et al., 1979).

CHANGES IN CSF

The concentrations of HVA and 5-HIAA were reduced in CSF from patients with a provisional clinical diagnosis of Alzheimer's disease and an inverse relationship is found between HVA concentration and the degree of dementia (Gottfries et al., 1969a, b; Gottfries and Roos, 1976). Also, the increase in the concentration of 5-HIAA after probenecid was significantly lower in Alzheimer's patients than in age-matched controls (Gottfries et al., 1974). However, it is unclear whether histological identification of definite Alzheimer's disease was made in these studies and furthermore, there are many difficulties inherent in the interpretation of CSF data (Curzon, 1976). Thus the relevance of these interesting results to the pathogenesis of Alzheimer's disease is unclear.

PROTEIN SYNTHESIS

The protein synthesizing capacity of microsomal preparations of frontal grey biopsy material from two patients with Alzheimer's disease appeared normal (Suzuki *et al.*, 1964). These data are difficult to interpret as glial hyperactivity occurs which could mask changes in nerve cells. Mann and Sinclair (1978) find that cell ribosomal RNA and nucleolar volume are reduced in Alzheimer's disease, and summarize evidence that this may reflect depressed protein synthesis.

BLOOD FLOW AND ENERGY METABOLISM

In patients described as having 'chronic brain syndrome and psychosis' early studies demonstrated significantly low cerebral oxygen and glucose consumption (Sokoloff, 1976). Measurement of cerebral blood flow by the intracarotid radioactive xenon technique (Hachinski *et al.*, 1975) showed significantly low amounts of tissues which cleared xenon rapidly (largely grey matter), in multi-infarct dementia but not in presumed Alzheimer's dementia. These low values in the former group were probably due to the presence of an appreciable proportion of infarcted tissue. In later stages of senile dementia cerebral flow changes are markedly low (Ingvar and Gustafson, 1970), presumably because of brain atrophy.

There is neurophysiological evidence (Ingvar *et al.*, 1975) of subnormal function of the cortex in Alzheimer's disease. The blood flow to the grey matter was significantly reduced, especially in the occipital-parieto-temporal regions. The augmentation of flow in demented patients in the association areas during attempted activation by reading and psychological tests was less than normal and in some cases the blood flow was diminished. Such alterations in blood flow are related to vasodilation induced by carbon dioxide released by the increased metabolic activity of the neurons (Siesjo, 1977). There is evidence of reduced cerebral oxygen uptake in dementia (Grubb *et al.*, 1977). These may be important findings as reduced acetylcholine synthesis occurs when glucose oxidation is impaired by mild hypoxia (Gibson and Blass, 1976).

SUMMARY AND CONCLUSIONS

The cholinergic system appears to be especially affected at an early stage in the pathogenesis of Alzheimer's disease, as CAT activity is markedly low in biopsy specimens and in post-mortem material (Bowen *et al.*, 1979). These observations, and the relationships between CAT activity, senile degeneration and mental state, and also the response of early Alzheimer cases to 'cholinergic therapy' (Etienne *et al.*, 1978; Signoret *et al.*, 1978; Smith and Swash, 1979) all suggest that the low CAT activity is of clinical significance. As this could result from decreased nerve impulse activity (Tuček, 1978; Burgess *et al.*, 1978; Gottesfeld *et al.*, 1978) which may occur in Alzheimer's disease, it may be that the low CAT activity is a secondary effect. The most plausible interpretation, however, is that the low activity reflects the structural disintegration of the brain. No other reliable specific marker of nerve terminals has been measured in the temporal lobe. Although GAD activity may be spared (Bowen *et al.*, 1976a; Davies and Maloney, 1976; Spillane *et al.*, 1977; Reisine *et al.*, 1978) 5-HT and GABA receptive cells appear to degenerate. Therefore, more work is needed to establish whether the cholinergic system is selectively affected in Alzheimer's disease.

Although biochemical studies may identify important transmitter changes relevant to therapy, our data and those of others are based on an exact histological diagnosis. The likely success of therapy based on these and similar findings (Smith and Swash, 1978) is difficult to assess, for in any group of demented persons with cerebral atrophy there is no certain clinical way to identify those with Alzheimer's disease.

As CAT activity is probably not the rate limiting factor in acetylcholine synthesis (Tuček, 1978) a question which still remains to be investigated is whether or not this synthesis is reduced in the Alzheimer brain.

REFERENCES

Adolfsson, R., Gottfries, C. G., Oreland, L., Roos, B. E., and Winblad, B. (1978) Reduced levels of catecholamines in the brain and increased activity of monoamine oxidase in platelets in Katzman, R., Terry, R. D., and Blick, K. L. (eds.) *Alzheimer's disease: therapeutic implications, Alzheimer's Disease: Senile Dementia and Related Disorders: Aging,* Raven Press, New York, vol. 7, pp. 441–451.

Ball, M. J. (1977) Neuronal loss, neurofibrillary tangles and granulovacuolar degeneration in the hippocampus with aging and dementia. A quantitative study. *Acta Neuropath. (Berlin),* **37**, 111–118.

Ball, M. J. (1978) Topographic distribution of neurofibrillary tangles and granulovacuolar degeneration in hippocampal cortex of aging and demented patients. A quantitative study, *Acta Neuropath. (Berlin),* **42**, 73–80.

Berger, B., Escourolle, R., and Moyne, M. A. (1976) Axones catecholaminerques du cortex cérébral humain. *Rev. Neurol. (Paris),* **136**, 183.

Blackwood, W., and Cumings, J. N. (1959) Diagnostic cortical biopsy—an histological and biochemical study, *Lancet,* ii, 23–24.

Bowen, D. M., Smith, C. B., and Davison, A. N. (1973) Molecular changes in senile dementia. *Brain,* **96**, 849–856.

Bowen, D. M., and Davison, A. N. (1974) Macrophages and cathepsin A activity in human brain. *J. Neurolog. Sci.,* **21**, 227–231.

Bowen, D. M., and Davison, A. N. (1978) Biochemical changes in the normal aging brain and in dementia, in Isaacs, B. (ed.) *Recent Advances in Geriatric Medicine (I)* Churchill-Livingstone, Edinburgh, pp. 41–60.

Bowen, D. M., Smith, C. B., White, P., and Davison, A. N. (1976a) Neurotransmitter-related enzymes and indices of hypoxia in senile dementia and other abiotrophies. *Brain*, **99**, 459–496.

Bowen, D. M., Goodhardt, M. J., Strong, A. J., Smith, C. B., White, P., Branston, N. M., Symon, L., and Davison, A. N. (1976b) Biochemical indices of brain structure, function and 'hypoxia' in cortex from baboons with middle cerebral artery occlusion. *Brain Res.*, **117**, 503–507.

Bowen, D. M., Smith, C. B., White, P., Goodhardt, M. J., Spillane, J. A., Flack, R. H. A., and Davison, A. N. (1977a) Chemical pathology of the organic dementias (I), validity of biochemical measurements on human post-mortem brain specimens. *Brain*, **100**, 397–426.

Bowen, D. M., Smith, C. B., White, P., Flack, R. H. A., Carrasco, L. H., Gedye, J. L., and Davison, A. N. (1977b) Chemical pathology of the organic dementias (II), quantitative estimation of cellular changes in post-mortem brains. *Brain*, **100**, 427–453.

Bowen, D. M., White, P., Spillane, J. A., Goodhardt, M. J., Curzon, G., Iwangoff, P., Meier-Ruge, W., and Davison, A. N. (1979) Accelerated aging or selective neuronal loss as an important cause of dementia? *Lancet*, **i**, 11–14.

Bray, D., and Brownlee, S. M. (1973) Peptide mapping of proteins from acrylamide gels. *Anal. Biochem.*, **55**, 213–221.

Burgess, E. J., Atterwill, C. K., and Prince, A. K. (1978) Choline acetyltransferase and the high affinity uptake of choline in corpus striatum of reserpinised rats. *J. Neurochem.*, **31**, 1027–1033.

Cherayil, G. D. (1969) Estimation of glycolipids in four selected lobes of human brain in neurological diseases. *J. Neurochem.*, **16**, 913–920.

Corsellis, J. A. N. (1962) *Mental Illness and The Aging Brain*, Maudsley Monograph No. 9, Oxford University Press, Oxford.

Corsellis, J. A. N. (1976) Aging and the dementias, in Blackwood, W., and Corsellis, J. A. N., (ed.) *Greenfields Neuropathology*, Edward Arnold, London, pp. 796–849.

Crapper, D. R., Krishnan, S. S., and Quittkat, S. (1976) Aluminium neurofibrillary degeneration and Alzheimer's disease. *Brain*, **99**, 67–80.

Curzon, G. (1976) Transmitter amines in brain disease, in Davison, A. N. (ed.) *Biochemistry and neurological disease* J. Blackwell Scientific Publications, Oxford, p. 168.

Davies, P., and Maloney, A. J. F. (1976) Selective loss of central cholinergic neurones in Alzheimer's disease. *Lancet*, **ii**, 1403.

Davies, P., and Verth, A. H. (1978) Regional distribution of muscarinic acetylcholine receptor in normal and Alzheimer's-type dementia brains. *Brain Res.*, **138**, 385–392.

Etienne, P., Gauthier, S., Dastoor, D., Collier, B., and Ratner, J. (1978) Lecithin in Alzheimer's disease. *Lancet*, **ii**, 1206.

Fahrenkrug, J., Schaffalitzky de Muckadell, O. B., and Fahrenkrug, A. (1977) Vasoactive intestinal polypeptide (V.I.P.) in human cerebrospinal fluid. *Brain Res.*, **124**, 581–584.

Friede, R., and Magee, K. R. (1962) Alzheimer's disease: presentation of a case with pathologic and enzymatic-histochemical observations. *Neurology*, **12**, 213–222.

Friede, R. (1965) Enzyme histochemical studies of senile plaques. *J. Neuropath. Exp. Neurol.*, **24**, 477–491.

Gibson, G., and Blass, J. P. (1976) A relation between $(NAD^+)/(NADH)$ potentials and glucose utilization in rat brain slices. *J. Biol. Chem.*, **251**, 4127.

Goodhart, M. J., Strong, A. J., Bowen, D. M., White, P., Branston, N. M., Symon, L., and Davison, A. N. (1977) Effect of middle cerebral artery occlusion in baboon on neurotransmitter uptake and neurotransmitter-related biosynthetic enzyme activity. *Biochem. Soc., Trans.*, **5**, 160–163.

Gottesfeld, Z., Kvetňanský, R., Kopin, I. J., and Jacobowitz, D. M. (1978) Effects of repeated immobilization stress on glutamate decarboxylase. *Brain Res.*, **152**, 374–378.

Gottfries, C. G., Gottfries, I., and Roos, B. E. (1969a) The investigation of homovanillic acid in the human brain and its correlation to senile dementia. *Brit. J. Psychiat.*, **115**, 563–574.

Gottfries, C. G., Gottfries, I., and Roos, B. E. (1969b) HVA and 5-HIAA in the CSF of patients with senile dementia, presenile dementia and parkinsonism. *J. Neurochem.*, **16**, 1341–1343.

Gottfries, C. J., Kjällquist, A., Pontin, U., Roos, B. E., and Sundarg, G. (1974) CSF, pH and monoamine and glycolytic metabolites in Alzheimer's disease. *Brit. J. Psychiat.*, **124**, 280–287.

Gottfries, C. G. and Roos, B. E. (1976) Monoamine metabolites in cerebrospinal fluid in patients with organic presenile and senile dementias. *Akt. geront.*, **6**, 37–42.

Grossfeld, R. M., and Shooter, E. M. (1971) Study of the changes in protein composition of mouse brain during ontogenetic development. *J. Neurochem.*, **18**, 2265–2277.

Grubb, R. L., Raichle, M. E., Gado, M. H., Eichling, J. O., and Hughes, C. P. (1977) Cerebral blood flow, oxygen utilization and blood volume in dementia. *Neurology*, **27**, 905–910.

Hachinski, V., Iliff, L. D., Zilhka, E., du Boulay, G. H., McAllister, V. L., Marshall, J., Ross Russell, R. W., and Symon, L. (1975) Cerebral blood flow in dementia. *Arch. Neurol.*, **32**, 632–637.

Ingvar, D. H., and Gustafson, L. (1970) Regional blood flow in organic dementia with early onset. *Acta Neurol. Scan*, **Suppl. 43**, **46**, 42–73.

Ingvar, D. H., Risberg, J., and Schwartz Martin, S. (1975) Evidence of subnormal function of association cortex in pre-senile dementia. *Neurology*, **25**, 964.

Ishii, T. (1969) Enzyme histochemical studies of senile plaques and the plaquelike degeneration of arteries and capillaries. *Acta Neuropath., (Berl.)*, **14**, 250–260.

Ishii, T., and Haga, S. (1976) Immuno-electron microscopic localisation of immunoglobulins in amyloid fibril of senile plaques. *Acta Neuropath., (Berl.)*, **36**, 243–250.

Katzman, R. (1976) The prevalence and malignancy of Alzheimer's disease. *Arch. Neurol.*, **33**, 217–218.

Krigman, M. R., Feldman, R. G., and Bensch, K. (1965) Alzheimer's pre-senile dementia. A histochemical and electron microscopic study. *Lab. Invest.*, **14**, 381–396.

Lange, H., Thorner, G., Hopf, A., and Schroder, K. F. (1976) Morphometric studies of the neuropathological changes in choreatic diseases. *J. Neurolog. Sci.*, **28**, 401–425.

Ledeen, R. W. (1978) Ganglioside structures and distribution: are they localized at the nerve ending? *J. Supramol. Struc.*, **8**, 1–17.

Legros, J. J., Gilot, P., Seron, X., Claessens, J., Adam, A., Moeglen, J. M., Audibert, A., and Berchier, P. (1978) Influence of vasopressin on learning and memory. *Lancet*, i, 41–42.

Mann, D. M. A., and Sinclair, K. G. A. (1978) The quantitative assessment of lipofuscin pigment, cytoplasmic RNA and nucleolar volume in senile dementia. *Neuropath. App. Neurobiol.*, 4, 129–135.

Miyakawa, T., Sumiyoshi, S., Murayama, E., and Deshimaru, M. (1974) Ultrastructure of capillary plaque-like degeneration in senile dementia. *Acta. Neuropath. (Berlin)*, 29, 229–236.

Nikaido, T., Austin, J., Trueb, L., and Rinehart, R. (1972) Studies in the aging of the brain II, microchemical analyses of the nervous system of Alzheimer's patients. *Arch. Neurol.*, 27, 549–554.

Niklowitz, W. J. (1975) Neurofibrillary changes after acute experimental lead poisoning. *Neurology*, 25, 927–934.

Oliveros, J. C. Jandali, M. K., Timsit-Berthier, M., Remy, R., Benghesal, A., Audibert, A., and Moeglen, J. M. (1978) Vasopressin in amnesia. *Lancet*, i, 42.

Perry, E. K., Perry, R. H., Blessed, G., and Tomlinson, B. E. (1977a) Necropsy evidence of central cholinergic deficits in senile dementia. *Lancet*, i, 189.

Perry, E. K., Perry, R. H., Gibson, P. H., Blessed, G., and Tomlinson, B. E. (1977b) A cholinergic connection between normal aging and senile dementia in the human hippocampus. *Neurosci. Letters*, 6, 85–89.

Perry, E. K., Perry, R. H., Blessed, G., and Tomlinson, B. E. (1978a) Changes in brain cholinesterases in senile dementia of Alzheimer type. *Neuropath. Appl. Neurobiol.*, 4, 273–277.

Perry, E. K., Tomlinson, B. E., Blessed, G., Bergmann, K., Gibson, P. H., and Perry, R. H. (1978b) Correlation of cholinergic abnormalities with senile plaques and mental test scores in senile dementia. *Brit. Med. J.*, ii, 1457–1459.

Peters, T. J. (1977) Application of analytical subcellular fractionation techniques and tissue enzymic analysis to the study of human pathology. *Clinical Science and Molecular Medicine*, 53, 505–511.

Puszkin, S., Nicklas, W. J., and Berl, S. (1972) Actomyosin-like protein in brain: subcellular distribution. *J. Neurochem.*, 19, 1319–1333.

Reisine, T. D., Bird, E. D., Spokes, E., Enna, S. J., and Yamamura, H. I. (1978) Pre- and post-synaptic neurochemical alterations in Alzheimer's disease. *Trans. Am. Soc. Neurochem.*, 9, 203.

Scheibel, A. B., and Tomiyasu, U. (1978) Dendritic sprouting in Alzheimer's presenile dementia. *Exp. Neurol.*, 60, 1–8.

Shelanaski, M. L. (1978) Discussion, in Katzman, R., Terry, R. D., and Bick, K. L. (eds.) *Alzheimer's disease, senile dementia and related disorders: Aging*, Raven Press, New York, vol. 7, p. 429.

Siesjo, B. K. (1977) Physiological aspects of brain energy metabolism, in Davison, A. M. (ed.) *Biochemical Correlates of Brain Structure and Function*, Academic Press, London. pp. 175–209.

Signoret, J. L., Whiteley, A., and Lhermitte, F. (1978) Influence of choline on amnesia in early Alzheimer's disease. *Lancet*, ii, 837.

Smith, C. B., Bowen, D. M., and Davison, A. N. (1974) Loss of a specific protein from brain in dementia. *Biochem. Soc. Trans.*, 2, 661–663.

Smith, C. B. (1976) *Neurochemical correlates of brain degeneration in senile dementia*. Ph.D. Thesis, University of London.

Smith, C. B., and Bowen, D. M. (1976) Soluble proteins in normal and diseased human brain. *J. Neurochem.*, 27, 1521–1528.

Smith, C. M., and Swash, M. (1978) Possible biochemical basis of memory disorder in Alzheimer's disease. *Ann. Neurol.*, 3, 471–473.

Smith, C. M., and Swash, M. (1979) Physostigmine in Alzheimer's disease. *Lancet*, i, 42.

Sokoloff, L. (1976) Circulation and energy metabolism of the brain, in, Siegel, G. J., Albers, R. W., Katzman, R., and Agranoff, B. W. (eds.) *Basic Neurochemistry (2nd edn.)* Little Brown, Boston, pp. 388–412.

Spillane, J. A. White, P., Goodhardt, M. J., Flack, R. H. A., Bowen, D. M., and Davison, A. N. (1977) Selective vulnerability of neurones in organic dementia. *Nature,*.266, 558–559.

Stahl, W. L., Sumi, S. M., and Swanson, P. D. (1971) Subcellular distribution of cerebral cholesterol in cerebrotendinous xanthomatosis. *J. Neurochem.*, 18, 403–404.

Strong, A. J.,Goodhardt, M. J., Branston, N. M., Bowen, D. M., and Symon, L. (1977) The relationship between intensity and duration of cortical ischaemia and reduction of synaptosomal uptake of neurotransmitter in baboons. *Acta. Neurol. Scan.*, 56, 372–373.

Suzuki, K., Korey, S. R., and Terry, R. D. (1964) Studies on protein synthesis in brain microsomal system. *J. Neurochem.*, II, 403–412.

Suzuki, K., Katzman, R., and Korey, S. R. (1965) Chemical studies on Alzheimer's disease. *J. Neuropath. Exp. Neurol.*, 24, 211–224.

Terry, R. D., Fitzgerald, C., Peck, A., Millner, J., and Farmer, P. (1977) Cortical counts in senile dementia. *J. Neuropath. Exp. Neurol.*, 36, 633.

Tomlinson, B. E., and Henderson, G. (1976) Some quantitative cerebral findings in normal and demented old people, in, Terry, R. D., and Gerschon, S. (ed.) *Neurobiology of Aging*, Raven Press, New York, pp. 183–227.

Tuček, S. (1978) *Acetylcholine Synthesis in Neurons*. Chapman and Hall, London.

Uemura, E., and Hartmann, H. A. (1978) R.N.A. content and volume of nerve cell bodies in human brain, I. Prefrontal cortex in aging, normal and demented patients. *J. Neuropath. Exp. Neurol.*, 37, 487.

White, P., Hiley, C. R., Goodhardt, M. J., Carrasco, L. H., Keet, J. P., Williams, I. E. I., and Bowen. D. M. (1977) Neocortical cholinergic neurones in elderly people. *Lancet*, i, 668–670.

White, P. (1978) *Nerve cell markers in Alzheimer's disease*, Ph.D. Thesis, University of London.

White, P., Bowen, D. M., and Davison, A. N. (1978) Alzheimer's disease: distribution of protein on sucrose density gradient centrifugation. *Acta Neuropath. (Berl.)*, 41, 253–256.

Wimersma-Greidanus, T. J. B., and de Weid, D. (1977) The physiology of the neurohypophysical system and its relation to memory processes, in Davison, A. N. (ed.) *Biochemical Correlates of Brain Structure and Function*, Academic Press, London, pp. 215–248.

The Biochemistry of Psychiatric Disturbances
Edited by G. Curzon
© 1980 John Wiley & Sons Ltd.

CHAPTER 8

Relationships between Neurochemical and Psychiatric Disturbances: New Developments

G. CURZON

Summing up the colloquium on which this book is based, Professor Eccleston said: 'What can be called the unitary hypothesis of biogenic amine function—the idea that each system has a specific and separate role—must surely be revised. It has led to the concept that psychiatric syndromes involve disturbances of one or other specific transmitter. However, it is clearly an over-simplification to believe that NA, DA, 5-HT, and also the newer peptidergic systems act independently. The brain consists not of isolated neuronal groups but of interconnected circuits involving different transmitters which are regulated by various control mechanisms. For example, the work of Olds (1977) and Crow (1973) shows that there are functional interrelations expressed at a behavioural level between the DAergic and NAergic systems. Work involving lesions in the 5-HT system shows the inhibiting influence of 5-HT neurons on DAergic function. Numerous other studies indicate functional interactions between different transmitters.'

Since these remarks were made it has become increasingly apparent that the activities of the brain do not only result from the action of isolated transmitter systems. Animal experiments show transmitters acting in unison to give rise to numerous patterns of behaviour. Green and Grahame-Smith (1978) had already reported that the behavioural response to 5-HT receptor activation was influenced by drugs affecting catecholamine and GABA-containing systems. Their group had also shown that giving the 5-HT precursor L-tryptophan or the catecholamine precursor L-Dopa, after monoamine oxidase inhibitor pretreatments, elicited patterns of behaviour which (though different) had considerable similarities (Heal et al., 1976; Deakin and Green, 1978). More recently, work on drugs which caused backward-walking and circling showed that this occurred when 5-HT and DA were simultaneously released (Curzon et al., 1979; Fernando et al., 1980) and that it was influenced by drugs affecting NAergic, and GABAergic systems (J. C. R. Fernando and G. Curzon, unpublished work).

The components of the above behavioural pattern and of 'classical' 5-HT-provoked behaviour (involving reciprocal forepaw treading, hind-limb abduction, 'wet dog' shakes, etc.) exhibit different kinds of dependence on DA. For example, reciprocal forepaw treading was increased but 'wet dog' shakes decreased when DA tracts were destroyed by nigral lesions (C. D. Andrews, J. C. R. Fernando, and G. Curzon, unpublished work). Somewhat similarly, 'classical' DA-dependent behaviours (rearing, gnawing) caused by amphetamine at high dosage were increased but other behaviours (backward-walking, circling) decreased by 5-HT receptor blockade (Lees *et al.*, 1979). These relatively crude animal experiments show that transmitters can act in concert. They also illustrate that functional relationships between transmitters cannot be treated entirely in terms of actions on broad behavioural categories such as activity, arousal or stereotypy and that analogies with balance beams, switches, or gain knobs are inadequate.

The above conditions have implications for the study and treatment of psychiatric disorders. They suggest that similar psychiatric disturbances in different subjects might result from abnormalities of different transmitters and that a psychiatric disturbance in an individual subject might result from abnormalities of more than one transmitter. These considerations suggest multiple possibilities for therapeutic intervention using drugs which interact with different transmitter systems. Thus, drugs which appear to specifically affect either 5-HT or NA-containing systems are both effective in the treatment of depression (Baumann and Maitre, 1979; Bridges and Barnes, 1978; Stone, 1979). Furthermore, the DA agonist piribedil is reported to be antidepressant in some subjects (Post *et al.*, 1978). It is of particular interest that there was a significant negative correlation between CSF HVA concentration and therapeutic response. This suggests that a subgroup of depressives may exist who have defective DAergic function and therefore respond to DA receptor stimulation.

Recent work on 'trace amines' and depression should also be mentioned, i.e. the evidence of low urinary excretion of octopamine and tyramine metabolites and of low CSF concentration of phenylacetic acid, a metabolite of phenylethylamine which is a precursor of these amines (Sandler *et al.*, 1979a,b).

Recent discussions of transmitter abnormalities in schizophrenia (Joseph *et al.*, 1979; Van Kammen, 1979) emphasize the important role of DAergic hyperactivity but also suggest that disturbances of other transmitters may be important. We have suggested a possible role for 5-HT on the basis of observations that (a) rats exhibit backward-walking when given drugs which release catecholamines and 5-HT concurrently, and (b) many drugs which cause this behaviour in the rat are hallucinogens and/or cause schizophrenia-like states in man (Curzon *et al.*, 1979, 1980). Amphetamine is a notable example (Snyder, 1953; Woodrow *et al.*, 1978). Fenfluramine also causes backward-walking (Taylor *et al.*, 1974; Curzon *et al.*, 1979) and can lead to hallucinations and psychotic behaviour in man (Shannon *et al.*, 1974; Griffith *et al.*, 1975). Many other hallucinogens cause backward-walking (and circling) in animals, e.g. *p*-methoxyamphetamine, psilocybin, LSD, mescaline, and the hallucinogenic morphine mixed agonist/antagonist drugs cyclazocine, penta-zocine, and levallorphan (Smythies *et al.*, 1967; Schneider, 1968), while pheny-lethylamine which precipitates a proposed animal model for schizophrenia (Borison *et al.*, 1977) also causes backward-walking (Diamond and Borison, 1978). It may also be relevant that injecting 5-HT into the antero-ventral part of the cat caudate causes backward-walking and hallucination-like activity, i.e. behaviour interpretable as hunting and killing of non-existent prey (Cools, 1973).

Before the DA hypothesis came into favour the idea that an indoleamine disturb-ance was important in schizophrenia received much attention but well-defined positive findings were not reported (Weil-Malherbe, 1978) until recently when Sedvall (1980) obtained evidence suggesting raised 5-HT turnover in familial schizo-phrenia and Enna (1980) found that LSD-binding sites were deficient in autopsy brain material from schizophrenics. It is as yet unclear whether the latter abnormality occurs in the familial disease. The reported association between psychotic behaviour and urinary excretion of the hallucinogenic indoleamine dimethyltryptamine (Murray *et al.*, 1979) is another indication of disordered indole metabolism in schizo-phrenia, although its significance at present is obscure. It may be that schizophrenia in some subjects is associated not only with DAergic overactivity but also with a disturbance of 5-HT or some other indoleamine which exacerbates symptoms of the disease or has some permissive role in its behavioural expression.

Increased 5-HT turnover and decreased LSD binding sites in schizophrenia could be causally related. For example, the abnormality of turnover could be the primary disturbance and lead to a compensatory but ineffective receptor change or the receptor change could be primary and lead to a compensatory increase of turnover. These considerations have therapeutic implications—the suggestion has already been made that some neuroleptics owe their beneficial effect to antagonism at 5-HT receptors as well as at DA receptors (Leysen *et al.*, 1978). The therapeutic action of propranolol in schizophrenia may also be due to 5-HT antagonism (see Chapter 4).

It is clear that interest in the significance of 5-HT in schizophrenia has recently become reactivated. An alternative hypothesis on its role has been proposed based on evidence consistent with an association between reduced 5-HTergic activity and hallucinations (Jacobs, 1978). It was therefore suggested that amphetamine psychosis (and hence schizophrenia) may similarly depend on a brain 5-HT deficiency as this occurs in rats chronically treated with the drug (Trulson and Jacobs, 1979).

Relationships between central transmitter systems and human mood and behav-iour can hardly be less manifold than those now becoming apparent between trans-mitters and motor behaviour in laboratory animals. Nevertheless, it should not be assumed that the involvement of transmitters in psychopathology must invariably be complex. It may well be that some sharply circumscribed psychiatric disorders are mediated by transmitter abnormalities which are comparably narrowly defined. Possible examples are provided by certain monosymptomatic psychoses which tempt non-neurochemical interpretations but which are strikingly alleviated by the specific DA antagonist pimozide (Riding and Munro, 1975; Reilly *et al.*, 1978). However,

the existence of successful physical treatments of psychiatric illness does not necessary eliminate other methods from serious consideration. Indeed, the dividing line
between physical and other kinds of treatment may appear less sharp as we learn
more about the effects of environmental change and learning on central transmitter
systems.

REFERENCES

Baumann, P. A., and Maitre, L. (1979) Neurochemical aspects of maprotiline
    (Ludiomil). *J. Int. Med. Res.*, 7, 391–400.
Borison, R. L., Havdala, H. S., and Diamond, B. I. (1977) Chronic phenylethyla-
    mine stereotypy in rats: a new animal model for schizophrenia. *Life Sci.*, 21,
    117–122.
Bridges, P. K., and Barnes, T. R. E. (1978) New antidepressant drugs. *J. Pharma-
    cotherap.*, 1, 12–19.
Cools, A. R. (1973) Serotonin: a behaviourally active compound in the caudate
    nucleus of cats. *Israel J. Med. Sci.*, 9, Supp., 5–16.
Crow, T. J. (1973) Catecholamine containing neurones and electrical self-stimulation:
    (2). A theoretical interpretation and some psychiatric implications. *Psychol.
    Med.*, 3, 66–73.
Curzon, G., Fernando, J. C. R., and Lees, A. J. (1979) Backward-walking and
    circling: behavioural responses induced by drug treatments which cause simul-
    taneous release of catecholamines and 5-hydroxytryptamine. *Br. J. Pharmac.*,
    66, 573–579.
Curzon, G., Fernando, J. C. R., and Lees, A. J. (1980) Behaviour provoked by
    simultaneous release of dopamine and 5-hydroxytryptamine: possible relevance
    to psychotic behaviour, in Usdin, E., Sourkes, T. L., and Youdim, M. B. H. (eds.)
    Enzymes and Neurotransmitters in Mental Disease John Wiley, Chichester (in
    press).
Deakin, J. F. W., and Green, A. R. (1978) The effects of putative 5-hydroxytryp-
    tamine antagonists on the behaviour produced by administration of tranylcyp-
    romine, and L-tryptophan or tranylcypromine and L-Dopa to rats. *Br. J.
    Pharmac.*, 64, 201–209.
Diamond, B. I., and Borison, R. L. (1978) A new putative regulator of the extra-
    pyramidal system. *Pharmacology*, 17, 210–214.
Enna, S. J. (1980) Drug and disease-induced alterations in brain serotonin receptors,
    in Haber, B. (ed.) *Serotonin: Current Aspects of Neurochemistry and Function*
    Plenum, New York, (in press).
Fernando, J. C. R., Lees, A. J., and Curzon, G. (1980) Differential antagonism by
    neuroleptics of backward-walking and other behaviours caused by amphetamine
    at high dosage. *Neuropharmac*, 19, 549–553.
Green, A. R., and Grahame-Smith, D. G. (1978) Processes regulating the functional
    activity of brain 5-hydroxytryptamine: results of animal experimentation and
    their relevance to the understanding and treatment of depression. *Pharmako-
    psychiat.*, 11, 3–16.
Griffith, J. D., Nutt, J. G., and Jasinski, D. R. (1975) A comparison of fenfluramine
    and amphetamine in man. *Clin. Pharmac. Ther.*, 15, 563–570.
Heal, D. J., Green, A. R., Boullin, D. J., and Grahame-Smith, D. G. (1976) Single
    and repeated administration of neuroleptic drugs to rats: effects on striatal

dopamine sensitive adenyl cyclase and locomotor activity produced by tranyl-cypromine and L-tryptophan or L-Dopa. *Psychopharmac.*, **49**, 287–300.

Jacobs, B. L. (1978) Dreams and hallucinations: a common neurochemical mechanism mediating their phenomenological similarities. *Neurosci. Biobehav. Rev.*, **2**, 59–69.

Joseph, M. H., Frith, C. D., and Waddington, J. L. (1979) Dopaminergic mechanisms and cognitive deficit in schizophrenia. A neurobiological model. *Psychopharmac.*, **63**, 273–280.

Lees, A. J., Fernando, J. C. R., and Curzon, G. (1979) Serotonergic involvement in behavioural responses to amphetamine at high dosage. *Neuropharmac.*, **18**, 153–158.

Leysen, J. E., Niemegeers, C. J. E., Tollenaere, J. P., and Laduron, P. M. (1978) Serotonergic component of neuroleptic receptors. *Nature*, **272**, 168–171.

Murray, R. M., Oon, M. C. H., Rodnight, R., Birley, J. L. T., and Smith, A. (1979) Increased excretion of dimethyltryptamine and certain features of psychosis. *Arch. Gen. Psychiat.*, **36**, 644–649.

Olds, J. (1977) *Drives and Reinforcements*. Raven Press, New York.

Post, R. M., Gerner, R. H., Carman, J. S., Gillin, J. C., Jimerson, D. C., Goodwin, F. K., and Bunney, W. E. (1978) Effects of a dopamine agonist piribedil in depressed patients. Relationship of pretreatment homovanillic acid to antidepressant response. *Arch. Gen. Psychiat.*, **35**, 609–615.

Reilly, T. M., Jopling, W. H., and Beard, A. W. (1978) Successful treatment with pimozide of delusional parasitosis. *Brit. J. Dermatol.*, **98**, 457–459.

Riding, B. E. J., and Munro, A. (1975) Pimozide in monosymptomatic psychoses. *Lancet*, i, 400–401.

Sandler, M., Ruthven, C. R. J., Goodwin, B. L., Reynolds, G. P., Rao, V. A. R., and Coppen, A. (1979a) Deficient production of tyramine and octopamine in cases of depression. *Nature*, **278**, 357–358.

Sandler, M., Ruthven, C. R. J., Goodwin, B. L., and Coppen, A. (1979b) Decreased cerebrospinal fluid concentration of free phenylacetic acid in depressive illness. *Clin. Chem. Acta.*, **93**, 169–171.

Schneider, C. (1968) Behavioural effects of some morphine antagonists and hallucinogens in the rat. *Nature*, **220**, 586–587.

Sedvall, D. G. (1980) Serotonin metabolite concentrations in cerebrospinal fluid from schizophrenic patients: relationship to family history, in Haber, B. (ed.) *Serotonin: Current Aspects of Neurochemistry and Function*. Plenum, New York, (in press).

Snyder, S. H. (1973) Amphetamine psychoses: a 'model' schizophrenia mediated by catecholamines. *Am. J. Psychiat.*, **130**, 61–67.

Shannon, P. J., Leonard, D., and Kidson, M. A. (1974) Fenfluramine and psychosis. *Br. Med. J.*, iii, 576.

Smythies, J. R., Johnston, V. R., Bradley, R. J., Benington, F., Morin, R. D., and Clark, L. C. (1967) Some new behaviour-disrupting amphetamines and their significance. *Nature*, **216**, 128–129.

Stone, E. A. (1979) Subsensitivity to norepinephrine as a link between adaptation to stress and antidepressant therapy: an hypothesis. *Res. Comm. Psychol. Psychiat. Behav.*, **4**, 241–255.

Taylor, M., Goudie, A. J., Mortimore, S., and Wheeler, T. J. (1974) Comparison between behaviours elicited by high doses of amphetamine and fenfluramine: implications for the concept of stereotypy. *Psychopharmac.*, **40**, 249–258.

Trulson, M. E., and Jacobs, B. L. (1979) Long-term amphetamine treatment de-

creases brain serotonin metabolism: implications for theories of schizophrenia. *Science*, **205**, 1295-1297.
Vann Kammen, D. P. (1979) The dopamine hypothesis of schizophrenia revisited. *Psychoneuroendocrinol.*, **4**, 37–46.
Weil-Malherbe, H. (1978) Serotonin and schizophrenia, in Essman, W. B. (ed.) *Serotonin in Health and Disease*, Spectrum, New York, pp. 231-291.
Woodrow, K. M., Reifman, A., and Wyatt, R. J. (1978) Amphetamine psychosis—a model for paranoid schizophrenia, in Haber, B., and Aprison, M. H. (eds.) *Neuropharmacology and Behaviour*, Plenum, New York and London, pp. 1-22.

Subject Index